Business Management Tips From a Quality Punk

First Edition

http://www.lulu.com

Contents

Dedication

This book is dedicated to my ever patient, selfless and beautiful wife, Susan.

It is dedicated to my mother and my father who taught their son and daughter about working hard, and how it is much easier with a sprinkling of humor.

It is dedicated to my mentors Stuart Swalwell and Dr. Peter Worthington, who introduced me to the works of Dr. Deming and who helped me realize that everything that I learned during my university business management classes was a complete waste of time.

Preface

I don't believe that when I was a child that I dreamed of becoming a specialist in the field of Quality Management. My parents say that my ambitions, when I was young, were to be a bank manager. My working life in business didn't start in the financial sector, however in a Quality function in a manufacturing plant around the age of sixteen, although I did leave that plant, I've never left working in the Quality realm, nor will I ever leave it.

Business and management has always fascinated me. I like working with people, I like solving problems and I have tremendous joy in helping others. My career has furnished my ambitions with the wonderful gifts of learning, travel, teaching and mentoring.

I have learned that Quality is a universal constant in business, whether in manufacturing or in the service sector. However "quality" isn't an easy subject or discipline to be involved in. I like to ask people, "What is quality?" it is a great question, and I do not believe that there is such a thing as providing wrong answers to this. We all see quality differently, as it is based on our own personal value set.

A little later in my career, I first really figured out what business was all about when I was first posed the question above, and I was then introduced to the works of Dr. W. Edwards Deming. I became addicted to learning more about his philosophies and applying them. I would then branch out and read works by other authors, always yearning to get a new insight, to make my job easier, to make things better at work and to allow me to achieve new successes.

As I started to run out of books to read, I found an opportunity to read the latest books on the subject of business and quality management, as they were coming off the printing press. I approached Quality World magazine in London, to become a book reviewer. Without any experience in writing or book reviewing, they said "yes". Granted this was a purely selfish action, as I wanted nothing more to gain new knowledge through these books. I did this for a few years, and even today I enjoy the challenge of summarizing a book in three hundred words or less.

During a vacation in Egypt in 2011, weeks after watching their cultural revolution on the evening news, I was using my downtime to read two books for the magazine. The first I read was great, the second wasn't so great. In fact I didn't like it very much, and I would inadvertently growl aloud as I was reading it. As my wife's relaxation on the sun lounger next to me on the beach, was interrupted by my animal noises of disdain for this book, she challenged me "well can you do any better? Could you do a better job of writing about quality?" I do like a challenge, and that day I completed my first three articles, that were later picked up and published in QualityDigest.com.

This book is my collection of written work published in a variety of different magazines around the world, however mainly from the wonderful *Quality Digest* magazine. These have been collated, as a result of many requests to do so from the contacts that I've been fortunate to make through my writing. I do thank my friend Ken Sturgeon for giving the gentle boot up the behind to get me motivated to do this.

I greatly appreciate anyone who takes the time to read my mainly petty and ill-informed, but sometimes amusingly written words. However what I appreciate even more, is anyone who connects with me, or has an experience to share with me after reading one of my articles. Without them, I would have stopped writing long ago.

This is not a "how-to" guide on quality, nor a text book on the topic, however a collection of my first few years of articles. It may not flow or have a connecting thread from section to section, however I do hope that it will be easy to pick up to read or you find some of my hints and tips on business or management improvement in here.

I call myself a "Quality Punk" and an "Improvement Ninja". I've never like the job titles that my employers have presented to me, and as I have a choice when it comes to describing myself when I write, I prefer these terms. I do so purely for a reaction. I find it stimulates the thought processes in individuals when I introduce myself as a "Quality Punk" or as an "Improvement Ninja". It allows me to start a conversation on quality, and importantly make a connection through a little humor.

Within this book you will learn what my definition is of a "Quality Punk" is, and perhaps at the end, you too may define yourself as one.

Paul Naysmith

Lafayette, Louisiana, USA

September 2013

List of Abbreviations

ASQ	American Society for Quality
BRICS	Brazil, Russia, India, China, South Africa
CEO	Chief Executive Officer
CQI	Chartered Quality Institute
CSR	Corporate Social Responsibility
CTQC	Critical to Quality Characteristic
DMV	Department of Motor Vehicles
HR	Human Resources
IRCA	International Register of Certified Auditors
ISO	International Standards Organization
KISS	Keep It Simple Stupid
LSU	Louisiana State University
MBA	Masters in Business Administration
NFL	National Football League
PDCA	Plan Do Check Act
QMS	Quality Management System
R&D	Research & Development
SKATE	Skills, Knowledge, Aptitude, Training, and Experience
SPC	Statistical Process Control
TPS	Toyota Production System
TQM	Total Quality Management
UK	United Kingdom
US	United States
USA	United States of America
VIP	Very Important Person
VP	Vice President

Are You a Quality Punk?

I'm here to bring on the Quality Punk scene for the 2010s.

In the mid 1970s to mid 1980s the Punk movement was an intensely bright burning star that fizzled out just as quickly as it came in. As I understand it, the Punk movement was the antidote to the excessive color and pageantry of the Glam Rock scene. Punk music was stripped back, rockin' in your face, with full-on aggression. If you were really good, the crowd would riot, and fights would instantly break out. Gobbing on your band (spitting in their face) was a sign of appreciation. Those were the days. In the UK, the timing of this new music scene was coincidental to political change and de-industrialization of the British landscape. Disillusioned youth and mass unemployment only heightened the anti-establishment Punk ethos, creating waves of shock across the world, whilst without a care; Punk was flicking the middle finger at authority.

By now (hopefully) you are wondering "where is he going with this column" and "what the heck has gobbing got to do with quality?" Good.

There was another subculture evolving at the same time, borne of an undercurrent of dissatisfaction and disbelief in the system. As with Punk, its popularity quickly grew, and then it sputtered out just as fast. I'm talking about the 1980s total quality management (TQM) wave, the 1990s ISO 9001 crowd, and the 2000s Six Sigma belts.

Punk died because it was a fashion; but the Punk ideology lived on. It is the same with quality fashions. Many have performed research or written very successful books on the latest quality fashion, and while those fashions will eventually die, quality thinking is eternal. Quality thinking is the philosophy of "what we've got here just isn't right" or "could we do things in a different and better way?" Well, I'm here to bring on the Quality Punk scene for the 2010s. But, please hold off from making an appointment at the hairdressers for a spiky blue-tipped Mohawk, as I would doubt you would be welcome in most boardrooms.

Let us start with the founding fathers of the Quality Punk scene: I can think of some great people through time that went against the grain, that didn't agree with the principles or thinking at the time, and subsequently we are still talking about their achievements today:

Galileo Galilei, father of modern physics and a Quality Punk. Through empirical observations he proved that the earth wasn't at the center of the universe. He is credited to be the first to employ the scientific approach of applying mathematics with experimentation. He is a Quality Punk, because his teachings were contrary to the teachings of the 17th century Church (BBC).

Sir Ronald Fisher, founder of modern statistical thinking and Quality Punk. By taking a systematic approach to "real" data, he created new statistical methods including analysis of variance and design for experiments. He is a Quality Punk, since he introduced a new theory to why civilizations fall (Encyclopeadia Britannica), going against then common ideas, using evidence from data he had.

Henry Ford, industrialist and Quality Punk. His philosophy was to pay high salaries to his employees, with the knowledge that they could buy his affordable automobiles. Quality Punk extraordinaire, he was the first to create an entirely plastic car (The Henry Ford) that would run on bio-fuel at the beginning of the 1940s.

I would have to admit that sometimes I choose not to take the conventional approach to business, and perhaps I see the world slightly differently than my colleagues.
Sometimes I've found that my quality idea would get lost or lose its impact if I didn't add a little "Punk" to it. As a well-trained Quality Ninja Assassin, you would no doubt agree that you have to be flexible in style, yet make a devastating killer impact when called to. A Quality Ninja has to carry weapons; these weapons are concealed and very sneaky. My weapon of choice: neon colored socks. Oh yeah, how Punk is that?

It's not how you wear the socks, however; it's when you deploy them. In my case, I cherished the meeting with Mr. "D" Manager to deploy the sock tactic. D is for Dominator. You know the type, the person who likes to use management buzz words like "two-way conversation,"... as long as both ways are his.

The first time I deployed operation "Neon Sock Punking" was in a meeting where Mr. D was giving his all, like an angry beaver biting at a tree trunk. I saw that he was passionate about actually wanting to make an improvement, but wasn't winning over some of the other stakeholders in the room. So I waited for the perfect moment to launch my secret weapon. In the middle of his arm waving and desk thumping I fawned the need to tie my shoe lace. As I am a giant stick insect of a man, I could easily lift my (praying mantis-like) leg and place the sole of my shoe on the chair seat, thus revealing my sock weapon. Trousers riding high up my shins, I exposed the retina scorching colors of my sock to everyone in the room. Mr. D's eyes locked onto this sock, transfixed like a stunned squirrel looking at a mighty oak bristling with nuts. I pounced into action in his momentary pause: "So we *agree* we need to move forward. Let us all *agree* on the appropriate actions and timelines. Wouldn't you *agree* Mr. D Manager?" Everyone, relieved that I had interjected, quickly agreed with what I said: I suspect just to get on with their day. Mr. D snapped out of his paralysis, all confused, as if woken from a dream. "Erm, what was I saying... yes, good plan Paul!" He was Quality Punked like a good 'un.

I have tried other Quality Punk approaches, and failed, however I have learned from them. What's good about taking the learning approach that I take is that I have to be innovative and creative all the time, and I cherish that challenge with all the wonderful managers I meet.

Quality improvement is about changing the status quo, and each approach will be different in any scenario or business. As someone once said "good, just isn't good enough." We have to move forward, because if we don't, our competition will stride out in front and our customers will raise their expectations beyond our reach. I have learned to not immediately follow whatever the latest fashion is, but to try to understand where it originated. It most cases, fashions do repeat themselves, whereas core values or philosophies are perpetual and need to be sustained. I only need to look at the recent high profile failures, created when core values were replaced by management working to the current fashion, to confirm my point of view.

To establish if you are a Quality Punk, please answer yes or no to the following questions:
• Have you ever challenged the "system"?
• Are you unlikely to believe what you are told or take things on at face value?
• Have you ever asked "Why"?
• Do you agree with continuous improvement for mutual benefit?
• Do you have a rockin' good time when making improvements?
• Would you agree that some quality professionals are slaves to ISO 9001 and forget why they are in business?
• Have you ever flicked the finger at the "man"?
• Do you have a tattoo of "PDCA," on your face or another visible body part?

• Have you ever spat in the face of a colleague, out of respect, for the work they have done?

 If you answered "No" to any of these questions, you are not a Quality Punk, and have some way to progress. However if you flicked the finger at the computer screen and shouted "I'm not going to work to your rules!" congratulations you are a Quality Punk in the 2010s.

In Search of the Good Mentors

Is there a correlation between retiring quality professionals and diminishing business competence?

If you're reading this article, especially in the United Kingdom, it's possible that you are a member of the Chartered Quality Institute (CQI). As I currently understand it, the average member is in her mid-50s, and therefore you may be looking not so far into the future to your retirement. You probably had, or currently are having, a successful career in the quality profession. However, if you look behind you, do you have someone competent to fill your shoes?

During the 10 years or so since I have been in business, I have to state that there are an ever-decreasing number of graduates in the United Kingdom coming from a technical background. Fewer and fewer science or engineering graduates are gracing the pages of recruiters, and as a result, this is a golden period for salaries in technical roles. Also in my opinion, the quality of these graduates is lower than when I graduated in 2000. If you are an average member, you would no doubt argue that even my generation of graduates were of a lower standard than yours.

So this poses a question for us quality or business professionals: Where do we expect our competent future replacements to come from? First, let's agree on what competence is. There exists a useful acronym, which simply sums up the elements of competence: SKATE, or skills, knowledge, aptitude, training, and experience. It is probable that you have some or all of these tenants of competence. However, if not, I firmly believe mentoring will guide those entering the profession toward achieving competence.

History and traditional tales have taught us that a wise mentor will help the hero overcome his enemy. We need new quality heroes to overcome a future of disappearing businesses, so where are these much-needed mentors to guide them? During this first recession of the 21st century, some well-reputed and sizable companies became extinct in the Western Hemisphere, and others are underperforming. Could there be a correlation between a generation of professionals retiring and a distinct lack of business competence left behind that's steering the ship toward uncertainty, and possibly even disaster?

Let me be the first quality professional to admit that I failed to prevent the recession from occurring. I now realize that I was not prepared yet to challenge the "system" and win, only prepared to work with it. With hindsight, I understand that I had not yet completed my quality apprenticeship from my mentor; I was not therefore competent to take on the system. My mentor showed me a path to follow, and taught me how to make informed decisions, all in the pursuit of knowledge, not for financial gain. I will also admit that I am not the finished article or the polished quality jewel because I have a lifetime of learning still to do. However, I do still have my mentor to show me leadership, and he keeps me focused on building on my competencies. For this I am eternally grateful.

As a way of honoring my mentor, I am following his example, and I also get great personal reward from mentoring others early in their quality careers. In many ways CQI has assisted me by providing a framework to guide newly initiated quality professionals to becoming chartered quality professionals.

Perhaps at this point you are thinking, "You're going to ask me to become a mentor" or, "I don't have a mentor; I need to go and seek one." I am not going to ask you to do either.

As a wise leader and mentor to man, once said: "Lack of knowledge... that is the problem." My call to action is to pick up a copy of *The New Economics,* by W. Edwards Deming (Deming, 2000). In chapter four, you will see that the first step in transformation is all about an individual's understanding of the system of profound knowledge. To me, this is where professional mentoring must begin and center around. Make today the starting point in the journey as a mentor and a mentee.

My Toyota Dilemma

Applying critical-to-quality characteristics on a subjective decision

As a quality professional, I am a huge admirer of what the Japanese, and in particular Toyota, have given the business world, and how they have influenced quality improvements like no other in history.

Although in recent years Toyota did have a "blip" in its immaculate history, according to the J. D. Power 2010 Initial Quality Study (J.D. Power, 2010), its cars still top surveys and polls for quality and reliability. Out of sheer respect for the Toyota approach or "way," when I teach people about quality, I tend to drop in Toyota examples. Afterwards my students ask me, "Which Toyota do you drive?" apparently looking for some advice on getting a good motor. My answer usually is, "Er... well... it's... I don't have one." Here I am, a quality professional singing Toyota's praises and not owning one. Do I thereby lose some credibility in front of my students? Perhaps you, too, are in a similar position as I: a quality professional with a Toyota dilemma.

As I write this, I am in the position of looking to replace my current European "people's car," which has led me to think about what my preferred Toyota option should be. So to start off, like any good quality professional, I need to understand my critical-to-quality characteristics. Perpetuating the Scottish stereotype, economy heads the list.

Why is economy my critical-to-quality characteristic? I live 30 miles from my place of work, and this means I have to do a lot of driving. I use so much fuel; I feel that I am personally funding the entire UK government through all the duty I pay. This leads me to consider one of those Toyota hybrid cars because they tend not to be heavy drinkers. However, to be honest, I couldn't bring myself to own one as they are just plain ugly.

Why is the way that a car looks important to me? Simply, I am vain and daft enough to think that a car is a reflection of me or my character. So for good looks, I'll need to explore something in Toyota's Lexus division of cars. After test driving a very aesthetically pleasing Lexus, I felt that the driving experience was a bit of a letdown.

Why is the driving experience important to me? Given that I do so much driving over a mix of country lanes, main roads, and motorways, I need to have some level of enjoyment in doing so. Sorry, Lexus; compared to your Munich-based competitor, you lose. However your German opposition is rather—in fact a lot—more expensive for the same specifications of a similar vehicle.

Why is the cost limiting my options? Like many others I'm working to a budget, which is determined by how much of a loan I can afford. So I have identified a better-value option, in my price range, which excludes the ultimate Bavarian driving machine as a choice.

So what is my Toyota option? It is something I use every day, it is super-powerful, and it will take me places quickly and effectively. I enjoy using it, showing it off to everyone I meet, and it brings tremendous value to me and others when used. I thank you, Japan and Toyota, for the vehicle I settled on: its simplicity is its beauty.

If you are still wondering what my preferred Toyota option is, you may wish to reflect on your career in quality. "Why?" you may ask—and so you should. Repeatedly.

Innovate Like a Movie Director

Why not get creative on an epic scale?

I love films. I just love that cinematic experience. It's the best experience you can have in a darkened room when someone has spent $200 million on two hours of entertainment. I often truly can't believe how creative and brilliant some minds are. Do you remember the last movie you saw and walked away from, lost for words to describe it? The last time I had a wide-eyed and excited feeling after a movie was from watching the British director Christopher Nolan's 2010 epic, *Inception*.

If you haven't yet seen it, I would strongly suggest that you consider making it an addition to your collection. The science fiction story is about a group of spies getting inside dreams to capture secrets. Doesn't sound like the making of a classic plot, and it's perhaps not a movie for those, like my ever-patient wife, who like period-costume crime dramas.

There is one notable scene that has some jaw-dropping special effects, where a good spy has a fight with a baddie in a hallway. On its own, this doesn't sound spectacular; however, the hallway at the time is spinning on its axis. Each agent is pitted against each other in mortal combat as the walls are turning to become the ceiling—and at some speed.

Being a problem-solver, I like to reflect on how this would or could be performed. During the last 25 years, computer graphics have been so influential in movie design; I presumed that was how Nolan created his vision for millions of the paying public to enjoy. So I felt resplendent with my assessment until recently, when I was proven wrong; it wasn't a computer generated special effect at all. I learned of my mistake when I was traveling by air about a year after the movie had been released. I managed to catch a "making of" documentary of the very scene I just described. In the documentary Nolan started with his vision on paper, and presented this comic book description to his top set and special-effect designer. Put yourself (if not already) in a high-pressure position in a creative industry that is highly competitive, always trying to outdo the last brilliant vision no one has seen before, and being faced with this huge challenge of making a hotel corridor spin on its axis with two actors inside. I would have to assume that only a master innovator and problem-solver could successfully face this challenge.

The solution was presented on the tiny screen in front of me at 30,000 feet up: Build a 100-foot corridor, in a frame that is rotated through 360° by powerful motors. It was massively complex and a huge engineering challenge that resulted in an awesome experience for the audience.

This got me thinking, a bit tangentially, on Darwinian principles. Would this expert special-effects wizard have innovated were it not for the working environment he was in? In the same way animals adapt and survive in their ecosystems, had this movie production, or system, allowed this innovation to be created?

When I realized how wrong my presumption was, I had a greater sense of awe after understanding how they did it. I was happy with the notion that I was wrong, but I was disheartened to think that I or the people I work alongside do not innovate on the same scale as the movie industry.

Please don't get me wrong. I *do* work in an innovative business. However most of the time it is innovation from people working in a broken system. What I mean is that workers find ways to work around the system, with the intent of attempting to achieve a positive outcome for the customer.

For example, in my past experience, an operator fashioned a tool (of sorts) out of a brush handle and other items available in his area. He made this "tool" to assist in a difficult task he was responsible for carrying out on a frequent basis. When learning of this, the engineers became concerned because it wasn't designed in accordance to some complex calculation that only engineers can comprehend. The manager was enraged because it was an unapproved technique. Only I was impressed with the ingenuity and drive of someone just wanting to do a quality job.

The issue is not with the operator or the tool but with the system that required time-consuming engineering, combined with a management organization that wouldn't listen or enable improvements in the workplace. This would only stifle, rather than encourage, innovation.

As for the operator, his natural problem-solving abilities were recognized and enhanced through training. This was achieved only through changing the system. The operator has gone on to become an excellent leader, and I hope he encourages others to come up with simple and practical solutions as he did.

Chris Corbould, the special-effects supervisor on the *Inception* production, had this to say of Nolan: "He extracts every drop of creative juice out of you and throws it in the film." Doesn't that sound like a rewarding way to work? Why don't you start behaving like a movie director and encourage a creative system where people are allowed to innovate freely on an epic scale?

Why I Wish I Got My Black Belt from Hong Kong Airlines

How cool would it be to kick your manager's butt?

I greatly believe in training. I have been fortunate to work in businesses that also believed in having trained and qualified professionals in their organization. I have personally and professionally benefited from that philosophy, and I have gained new knowledge as a result.

Since graduating from university, the most time-consuming and costly training I have been asked to undertake was my lean Six Sigma Black Belt training. The training comprised nearly 50 hours of e-learning, six residential sessions over six months, and submission of two projects demonstrating all the tools and techniques that I learned. The instructors were excellent, and often I was reminded that I was going to learn more than 140 tools and techniques during the course. I used this number to brag to others about how proficient I was going to become.

I don't think I have even 10 hand tools in my garage, but if having loads of hand tools makes an excellent garage, it follows that having lots of lean Six Sigma tools would make an excellent employee. After my training, though, I found that I favored techniques that were simple and effective. So taking a "lean" view of my skills, it could be argued that many of them were valueless since I was selecting and using only what would bring value.

OK, so I may not use 95 percent (or more) of the tools and techniques from my Black Belt training, but I have the potential to use them. Or do I? It has been five years since my training, and without practicing some very complex statistical analysis, I feel that this potential has been eroded.

This is why we need training and retraining continuously. For example, my first-aid certificate—also paid for by my employer—has an expiration date that encourages retraining to ensure I'm familiar with current life-saving techniques. However, even that has proved nonvalue added. During the nine years since my first-aid class, I've never had to use the knowledge in my workplace. In fact, I've used these skills only three times outside of work, and none of the incidents were life-threatening. For this case, though, it could be argued that it is better to have the training than not at all.

I often wonder if this argument holds true for other training. Is it really better to have than not have?

I regularly meet managers who complain that their people are "collecting" training certificates, insinuating that the training was unnecessary and somehow preventing business from happening. And I also hear training instructors complain about managers not attending scheduled training that would be of tremendous benefit to the business. However, in all cases of nonvalue-added training, the abuse of training or lack of it is due to the system that created it. As quality professionals, shouldn't we be asking what training is necessary in our processes that would add value for our customers?

Concerning this article's title, "Why I Wish I Got My Black Belt from Hong Kong Airlines": It's based on a report I read in *The Wall Street Journal* about a training program (Wall Street Journal, 2011) that Hong Kong Airlines is planning. According to the report, "the airline plans to make it mandatory for its cabin staff to undergo training in Wing Chun, a type of martial art often used in close-range combat" due to an "average of three incidents a week involving disruptive passengers." If you consider that in one week the airline moves more than 46,000 passengers, this is equivalent to one disruptive passenger per 15,000. If the average plane holds 300 people, that is one disruption per 50 journeys.

I would love to have been in the meeting when they assessed that Wing Chun was the best option as a mitigating action because I would have challenged it. I would have suggested an approach that considered ways to prevent a combative situation while simultaneously protecting the employee from any potential danger, rather than asking an employee to open a can of "whoop ass" on a customer. I theorize that one beaten-up customer would become one less repeat customer.

I may have created a contradiction here. I want to become proficient in Kung Fu, and my reason is simple: How cool would it be to have the opportunity to kick some manager's butt, on the instruction of your employer, all in the pursuit of education? However, this proficiency would not bring repeat custom, either. Nonetheless, in the Kung Fu class, I would tattoo "PDCA" across my knuckles. Why? Because I would definitely like to impress PDCA on Mr. Manager, only with repeated applications.

If Deming Could See What You're Doing...

When making a change shouldn't simply be copying someone else's idea

If W. Edwards Deming could see what you're doing, he'd punch you in the face. OK, not really. He may have been brutally honest in his lectures, but I don't think he ever punched anyone. However, he would have plenty to say about how often one business copies (I believe the term today is "benchmarks") the good ideas from another business with no thought about context. Why is it that if we hear about another organization's idea—particularly one that claims to have a positive influence on business performance—we'll try to copy it?

One of the maddest business-improvement ideas I've seen recently was "Take Your Dog to Work Day," which swept through U.S. workplaces on June 24, 2011. That story, all about the fully-flowing positivity of taking an animal to the office, was treated to a full-page spread in the *Guardian* (Guardian Newspaper, 2011). Included in bold typeface was a survey of 3,000 office workers conducted by the Bio Agency (why these outfits can't do research on something that might benefit all of humanity escapes me). Apparently 55 percent of those canvassed admitted they *would* feel more motivated if they had a pet in the office.

Before all you pet lovers (that does also include me) start sharpening your poison pens to respond, let me expand on why copying an improvement idea from one business to another is not always the best plan of action.

A good friend of mine likes to call me up occasionally to talk over "business." Once he asked for some advice when he was tasked to head an investigation that had been initiated in response to a customer complaint. The problem was so significant that my friend's company assigned him to lead a small team full-time, which took him away from his normal duties until the issue was fully resolved. From his investigation he found that the factors leading to the failure were many and complex.

Now and again, while he was struggling to see the end of the analysis tunnel, he'd remark that all he could see were problems layered on problems, and that he was just sinking deeper. So I would keep him focused on the "system" that created the failure, and ask why that system had not prevented the failure from escaping the factory gates. That he would reluctantly admit to this (a rarity because he's a stubborn chap), helped him significantly.

Over a beer and pizza sometime later, we caught up before his mammoth report, packed full of evidence, was due for submission to his upper management. Talking over the contributing factors to the problem, he described the sub-cause of the process failure. Our exchange went something like this:

"The assembly that the failure was centered around didn't get its final check before its dispatch on the late Friday afternoon pick-up," he explained.

"Why did that happen?" I asked.

"There were no technical approvers around to support and approve it, but because it was an urgent delivery, it had to go."

So we talked about why his organization delivers only on a Friday, the culture in the business, the methods used, and finally, the "system." I learned there were no technical approvers around because the company's "Human Remains" staff (his name for HR) changed the workday's policy for the technical department so it could have Friday afternoons off.

I sat there stunned, partly by what he said and partly because my brain was screaming that layers of taste buds were being melted off by the liquid magma cheese on the pizza crust. Then my mind flicked into gear like a race driver overtaking a rival at the Monaco Grand Prix. I framed the obvious question, which I managed to voice following the cooling effects of a glug of beer:

"So why would your HR give the tech guys Friday afternoons off if they are a part of the manufacture and delivery process?"

"Well, during the last year the technical department has lost a lot of engineers to companies on the north side of town," he said. "These places offer a similar salary package, but also a nine-day fortnight." This means that engineers at the other companies have every other Friday off work, or nine working days out of ten. Other than thinking that was a sweet deal, and how do I apply, I inquired, "So what's that have to do with your tech team?"

"The dead heads in Human Remains"—my friend clearly wasn't enamored by his company's personnel support— "wanted to stop the attrition by introducing the nine-day fortnight. Upper management wouldn't agree because we're active all through the working week, so the compromise was for half-day Fridays."

There you have it, a perfect example of why not to copy an idea that works for another company. Through not understanding the cause of staff turnover, management— with the best of intentions, I believe—made a change to improve the situation. But because the risks and potential impact of the change weren't assessed, business took a turn for the worse, which resulted in a customer complaint.

I've personally learned, at times the hard way, which you can't simply cut and paste from one business model to another.

Long ago, when consulting for Ford, Deming said, "American management thinks they can just copy from Japan—but they don't know what to copy." (Walton, 1998) His comment is as relevant today for my friend as it was for Ford. It's easy for anyone to emulate others in the short term; however, the true test is to learn for oneself. The rewards are far greater, and they last far longer.

Continuing with Deming, I mean no offense by this column's opening line. I believe that he was a peaceful individual and a generous soul. After reading Cecilia Kilian's *The World of W. Edwards Deming* (Kilian, 1992), I learned that he would donate his lecturing fees, during his travels in the 1950s in Japan, back into the improvement of that devastated country. My opinion that he was a brilliant philosopher was changed to believing he was a great human being.

And now to return to the idea of pets at work. Here's why it's mad: If I were to bring a box of kittens or puppies into your workplace, would you honestly focus on your customer that day?

Dr. Deming's Camping Expedition

In praise of cause and effect and 5 Whys

While playing her role as Maria Kutschera in *The Sound of Music*, Julie Andrews once sang about her favorite things, among which were geese flying with the moon on their wings, doorbells, and brown paper packages. Remembering these things were how Maria would distract herself when times were bad, a useful technique to deploy when being chased by Nazis across Austria with children in tow.

However, when things aren't going to plan at work, it's not kitten whiskers for me; its cause and effect diagrams and 5 Whys. You'd think that, with all their talent, Rogers and Hammerstein could have worked those into their tune. (And if you can fit quality tools and techniques into "My Favorite Things," by all means share your lyrics below; 100 Quality Kudos points for the best submission.)

I don't really remember the first time I applied or was involved in using these two tools. However, the power of each is the reason I still use them today.

The cause and effect diagram (or "fishbone diagram," as it's more popularly known) was the first quality control technique that really grabbed me. Its visual appearance drew me in, and I have to use it at least once a week or else I get withdrawal symptoms. It has always helped to put some order to my many thoughts and ideas.

Readers need to plough through nearly a quarter of Kaoru Ishikaw's *What Is Total Quality Control? The Japanese Way*

(Ishikaw, 1991) before they are introduced to the cause and effect diagram and approach. There they will find the author's musings over "the Ishikawa diagram," as Joseph M. Juran termed it. I recommend sneaking into a bookshop just to read that section for a giggle. You'll also find some amusing footnotes from the translator, who didn't entirely agree with Ishikawa's opinions.

I love the cause and effect diagram for its simplicity and near-zero cost to create, especially since it offers huge gains in conveying an idea or set direction. For example, I recently ran an experiment with a talented and qualified colleague. Not long out of academia, she was concerned about qualitative outputs, so we designed the experiment to provide both quantitative and qualitative results. Because she didn't know where to begin to collate the various feedback received, I suggested applying the cause and effect approach.

After the experiment had closed and all the results were received, I asked her to print and cut out each comment. (My office that day looked like the shredder had spewed its contents everywhere.) Using a flipchart, marker pens, and glue, we set out to collate the comments, now in little half-inch strips, into groups. Then each group was added to a branch of the diagram, poorly drawn by me on the flipchart. From this my colleague was able to see how a qualitative output moved to become something nearer to a quantitative form. She enjoyed both creating the diagram and the benefits gained from it, and has since become nearly as boring—er, productive—as I about using them.

A less well-known term for this technique is the "dog-bone diagram." It was coined when I was mentoring another colleague, who also went on to use it prolifically. At one point he had to demonstrate the cause and effect diagram to a group of operatives at a factory. Eyeing the image dubiously, their sarcastic spokesman concluded, *"Aye, it luks mair like a skeleton aff ae dug."* (Translated from

Scots: "Yes, it looks more like a skeleton off a dog.") Let's just say this operator came from the tougher side of town and could relate more to a dog's skeleton than a fish's. Since then I've cheekily taught some people the dog-bone diagram, purely for my own amusement.

You've got to love the simplicity of the 5 Whys concept. In *The Toyota Production System* (Ohno, 1988), Taiichi Ohno says, "To tell the truth, the Toyota Production System has been built on the practice and evolution of this scientific approach." Wow. So just by asking, "Why?" like an inquisitive toddler, Toyota conquered the world with high-value, low-cost vehicles? If it worked for them, it will surely work for you and me.

In my last chapter I warned of the dangers of thoughtlessly copying ideas from other companies, but this technique is the exception that proves that rule: Asking why all the time is the most effective route to overcoming problems. The only drawback to it I've found is when you've needed only three whys to get to the root cause, some determined people still go on to ask two more. Or else they stop at the fifth, even if they haven't gotten to the root cause. When I travel for work, people remember me as the guy who asks why a lot. I'm thinking about making a T-shirt emblazoned with, "Yes, why is my favorite question, and I'm about to ask it again." That might help cut out the small talk.

What I like about both techniques is that you don't need clever software, an abacus, or a calculator to use them. They are easy to teach to others and always create great value as an outcome. I like their simplicity. So Ishikawa and Ohno gave me my favorite quality tools. Not only that, they are also elements in my favorite W. Edwards Deming anecdote:

While on a busy lecture tour of Japan, Deming, along with a couple of good friends, took some time out to visit the beautiful Japanese countryside for a camping trip.

Late in the night, Deming awoke, and above him all the stars in the sky were twinkling down, as if a giant had cast a billion diamonds across the universe. Wide awake and cold, Deming saw that his two companions also were staring up at the sky.

"Iky?" Deming prompted his very good friend and translator, Ishikawa. "Lying here and looking up, what would be your empirical observation?"

"Well, I relate it to the five branches of a cause and effect diagram," Ishikawa replied. "Man: That is us three here together. Method: We're out camping. Material: the good food made on the campfire. Machine: Taiichi's reliable car that got us here. Mother Nature: at her most glorious all around us."

Deming rolled over and repeated the same question to Ohno.

"Deming," said Ohno, "with the majesty of the heavens above and the great expanse of the Milky Way, I'm reminded of the greatest question of all: 'Why?'"

Deming shook his head in disbelief at the two responses from his qualified and learned colleagues. "Blinded by the quality tools and techniques, you have missed the completely obvious," he fumed. "Someone has stolen our tent!"

Those Quality Magic Moments

Don't let them get buried and forgotten under everyday challenges

The human mind is currently the most intelligent device you will ever own. However, have you ever noticed how it has a filtering system? For example, do you remember the uneventful drive to the office this morning? I have no idea why the brain "forgets" these things, but in an instant you will be able to call on the memory of your first kiss.

I am a daydreamer; I could easily lose hours in a day just letting my thoughts and ideas freely roll around my head. Usually these are all about a problem I'm trying to solve. Can you recall when you last had a positive outcome at work? Perhaps you are lucky and have had a great many of these quality outcomes. I like to call them "magic moments."

Quite often I will return home after work, to be greeted warmly by my wife, who invariably asks how my day was. It's always an occasion when I can say, "Today I had a magic moment," and proceed to share my story with her.

My last quality magic moment occurred yesterday. I was in a meeting with two business managers who were providing me with an overview of their current business performance. This was the first time I had been to visit them, and during the presentation, they threw out a "data hand grenade." You know what I'm referring to here, data that are supposed to impress or bewilder you into silence. Often you'll hear the phrase "99.9-percent reliability." Being suspicious by nature, I heard in my head Kaoru Ishikawa advising, "If someone shows you data obtained by the use of measurement… consider them suspect."

What did they mean by 99.9-percent reliability? They should have known better than to toss that one directly at someone who studies and interprets data for a living.

This is where my magic moment began. Mr. Manager Jr. started by recounting how the team, under the stewardship of Mr. Manager Jr., identified each element of the process that had contributed to the customer's successes. In total the team had found 200 component parts of the process, and measured those against nine different measures of reliability. I know this doesn't sound particularly game changing, and many businesses do this every day. However, after being shown the detailed measurements, the magic moment presented itself to me through further explanation.

"Paul, before we started to measure all this, I thought it was a waste of time," Mr. Manager Jr. openly admitted to me. "Our competitors do not measure these things, and we thought, 'Why bother?'"

"So why did you measure it, then?" I inquired.

"Well, our customer wanted to know how reliable their process was, and we're a big part of it."

OK, I thought, you provided a figure to answer the client, which led me to ask, "Why continue measuring?"

Both managers smiled, and Mr. Manager Sr. followed with, "Now we don't need to sell the product anymore to the customer for repeat business because we're so dependable."

Being Scottish, I'm hard-wired to find negativity in everything, but that has stood me well in most improvement situations, so I continued: "Is there a risk that this level of repeatability cannot be sustained?"

This time the smiles were replaced by laughter. "We sustain reliability by using the measures to identify how to prevent failures," said Mr. Manager Sr.

Here was my magic moment. They had found the plan-do-check-act (PDCA) process without being taught it. They found it without a consultant teaching it, or without an army of quality professionals supporting it. How rare and wonderful a thing, a business that has evolved into having a world-class quality philosophy, and acting on it daily to their benefit, as well as their customer's and their customer's supplier's.

I like to collect these magic moments and use them whenever I'm faced with that difficult manager who thinks only about what quality improvements are going to cost, or when I'm told, "It can't be done" simply because no one has ever tried working in a different way.

Keep your magic moments close, share them with others on forums, blogs, and social networks, or pick up the phone and speak to someone. Share your magic moments not to brag, but to celebrate and inspire. If we don't impart them to others, it's quite possible our brains will filter them out, and they will end up as lost memories.

Life in a Technocracy

Technology has overcome problems I never knew I had

My wife and I were waiting near the departure gate at a miniature regional airport in Louisiana when the announcement blared: "Due to weather in Atlanta, your scheduled flight will not be disembarking for 15 minutes." Dismayed by the news, we exchanged worried looks and prepared for the worst. We had two further connections to make after Atlanta, where we'd be dealing with a layover of 1 hour and 20 minutes. It wasn't lost bags or missed connections that concerned us; it was the wedding in Scotland to which we'd been invited.

At this point in my career, having been through 15 countries on five different continents in the last four years, I've grown used to the experience of lost luggage. However, I've never lost a bag or missed a connection in the United States, so I was pretty confident we'd see our luggage at the other end, assuming we got there ourselves. Less fatalistic, my wife had her laptop out to check the times of the later connecting flights in Europe. "The next flight from Atlanta to Amsterdam is 8 hours after the previous," she reported. "We're not going to get to the wedding."

It was precisely at that point that a thought popped into my head, much like the old Microsoft paperclip help character used to tap on the screen to draw your attention. I know I should have been worrying about the wedding (and I carry some residual guilt about that), but I can't help it: I love to observe "the process" at all times. I'm sure that if I were allowed to, I'd draw a chalk circle around me at every opportunity, per Taiichi Ohno's philosophy, and happily stay in there for hours just watching and analyzing the world, considering what is good about it and what would need improving.

From my imaginary chalk circle at the airport, I saw that the waiting area was full of people with their heads down looking at bright little screens, the light reflecting in their eyes as they tried to find out why the flight was delayed or looked at their travel plans beyond Atlanta. Well, working in business for some time now, I appreciate that there can be an information lag when an electronic system isn't immediately updated by the meathead behind the computer, or because the meathead has incorrectly entered the data into the system.

This made me wonder why we, as a society, have become so reliant on technology for all the answers. Granted, technology has overcome problems I never knew I had, but why are we more likely to seek guidance from the Internet than from the employee at the desk? Have we become so accustomed to electronic devices that we've lost the ability to seek advice from, not to mention trust, the human elements of the system?

I'm very much aware that in business and industry, an army of inspector's checks goods on receipt, and auditors swarm over premises to confirm that someone neglected a requirement. However, most of us don't have the luxury of these resources in our personal lives, so perhaps leveraging technology gives us confidence in the uncertain world around us. As the old saying goes, "In God we trust; everyone else must bring data."

That still leaves some gaps, though. If I'm forced to trust "the machine," I do so never truly knowing where it gets its data from, or how accurate the information is. But unless I want to turn my back on the world and live in the wilderness, I must commit to implicitly trusting technology. When it's incorrect or lets me down, I must still accept it because I have only one way of discovering the errors: after the fact.

So to all the technology I rely on, here's my commitment to you:

To gas stations, I trust that your pumps will dispense premium rather than regular gas, and I trust that you will give me the volume I ask for. To my car, I trust that the speed you display is accurate, even though you're sometimes at variance with the speed displayed on my TomTom GPS. At least the two of you have never argued about it; I call that integrity.

To light switches, I trust you to provide the correct amount of electricity to the lamp to illuminate my darkness. You work every time I ask you to, and I never have to consider where you find your resources.

To my Snoopy watch, I've never calibrated you to confirm if even one minute of your time is the same as the atomic clocks'. But I still thank you for pointing to the positions on the dial to indicate the passing of time.

To my air conditioner, thank you for regulating the temperature to one-tenth of a degree accuracy, even though I don't think my body appreciates such subtlety.

To my refrigerator, thank you for reminding me I've left your door open too long by blinking and pinging at me, as I try to fill you with delicious contents.

Thank you, Google, for trying to finish my searches for me—without first asking—by giving me drop-down options, and for auto-filling the search boxes when I type in "why." It's as if you've read my mind.

I'm not mocking technology here, far from it: I'm one of the biggest tech-heads on the planet. But from time to time I like to try being a little less reliant on it to get me through the day. I like to see how different the world is when I make a phone call rather than sending an e-mail, try a face-to-face conversation rather than a phone call, or give up TV for a book. Sometimes I get very interesting results. Once I gave up the phone for a day, which forced me out onto the shop floor to speak to Mr. Manager. En route I got waylaid by an operator, who had an excellent solution to a problem we were working on.

"The last guy who did your job used to send 10 e-mails to us every day, and he never came out to see us," the operator commented. "Thank you for coming over." To this day he doesn't know I was on the way to see his boss. However, my giving up the phone made a positive change in his process and empowered him to make further changes.

As for the wedding I mentioned at the start of this ramble, we made all our connections, with technology's help, along with some added running through airports and lots of swearing. My bag wasn't as successful at making it on time, although my wife's was. This was the same bag that held my car keys. Keys for the car with my kilt locked inside, which I was going to wear to the wedding. My spare car keys, of course, languished at home, a 30-mile taxi ride away.

Like a crazy road movie, we eventually got to the wedding on time—which, at the end of the day and all philosophizing aside, was the important thing.

Quality in the Year 2022

Strategic planning forecasts from a wannabe futurologist

In the business world we certainly like to toss around choice words to express our ideas. I don't think I've ever used the term "strategic planning" in my home or personal life. I can well imagine my wife's stare of death (inherited from her two teacher parents) if I ever suggested that we "strategically plan our future." I'd get the stare not for suggesting we plan but for using meaningless business-speak just to say, "Can we talk about what we want to do later in life?"

When I run into strategic planning, it's usually attached to a decimal number of years. Perhaps you have 5-, 10-, or 15-year plans where you work. When we plan on serving new customers with new products in 10 years time, we can work back from that point and determine the steps needed to achieve these plans.

But being a systems thinker, I sometimes have the niggling thought that customers and the world around us will also be different in 5, 10, or 15 years, and I know that this will be outside my control. I often wonder what the world of quality will look like in 10 years. Will it be different, the same, or worse than it is today? Since I very much like the idea of being tagged a "futurologist," here is my take on the state of quality in 2022.

Apple tries electronic voodoo

On Halloween eve in 2022, Apple conducts a séance to contact Steve Jobs from the other side, hoping for assistance in launching its latest product: an electronic device so intelligent that humanity is no longer the cleverest thing on earth.

During the 10 years since Mr. Jobs' passing, consumers have become heartbroken, and Apple has floundered in the marketplace. The company has gone through 10 CEOs; increasingly desperate, the Apple board has resorted to black magic in an attempt to regain consumer trust. The board consults a voodoo high priestess, who burns herbs, falls into a trance, and intones, "Only Jobs do that job."

When the device is turned on at the launch, a message states, "New version available—click OK to upgrade." Upon upgrade, the super-intelligent machine declares that the word "genius" as applied to help staff at Apple retail stores greatly exaggerates their actual intellects. The geniuses say they prefer the previous version.

Four months later, Apple's competitors release a similar product, which starts a protracted legal case over patents, and an actual war breaks out.

Meanwhile, although humanity benefits from the improved logic of these devices, they cannot replace creativity. So the machines take over most of the logic chores, and company employees are paid to be creative at work. Innovation after innovation spread across the globe.

Colds and cancer cured; prescription prices skyrocket

After the cure for cancer and the common cold are found in 2017, the resulting treatments become the most expensive drugs in history. This forces the baby-boomer generation to work longer just to afford its medical bills. Realizing that there is an impending skills gap during the late 2020s as this generation begins to retire (the Retirement Act of 2021 has made it illegal to work beyond 80 years of age); the government decides to change its policy on immigration. Consequently, all borders are opened up without restrictions.

Back to the future—in 140 characters

A rejection of social networking websites becomes the norm due to over-advertising and corporate manipulation of companies like Face-Tube and TwitterGoogle. During the 2010s networking websites create a counter-culture where communities reject technology and actually meet face to face. However, spoken communication at these communal events is limited to 140 characters.

Charlie the Chart Reader is created

Scientific thinking is taught to kindergarten students. Statisticians, disappointed with the lack of chart analysis in the curriculum, create a super-brand of SPC for young students. It's a pink penguin called "Charlie the Chart Reader," which eventually becomes a wildly popular character on children's TV networks.

A cost-effective recession

3-D printers are proclaimed the cause of the worst recession of super-industrial powers—called "the BRICS"— ever recorded. With the improvement of design software and the very low cost of 3-D printers, it becomes more cost-effective to print a five-axis milling machine with built-in optical measurement, just to manufacture a single letter opener, than it is to walk to the store to buy one.

Quality cults and scams

Deming's four-day seminar is declared a cult, which subsequently creates such a media furor that the issue is discussed during a special meeting of the United Nations

General Assembly. Represented nations debate whether the seminar is a threat to their national policies on short-termism.

A management guru who released a book the year before is exposed as a fraud after an eagle-eyed reader notices that the author's breakthrough concept, called the "sword technique," is actually a repackaged 5-why approach.

ISO 9001:2020 is published

The ISO 9001:2020 revision is released in the spring of 2022, only two years late. This is an improvement of 18 months compared to the previous three revisions. This 2020 revision now has a revised model for quality where continuous improvement is integrated into the business and doesn't hang out to the side. The continuous improvement cycle retains its PDCA, but due to a corporate sponsorship deal with a soft drinks company, it is now known as Pepsi-Do-Cola-Again. This is also the first time that ISO gives away the standard for free on its website, and nonprofit organizations can benefit.

The 80 ISO-member countries that now contribute to the standard still can't agree to discuss merging other standards for safety or environmental systems.

Quality punks become historical curiosities

The Quality Punk movement of the 2010s starts to fade away, much like the neon color of the socks of the movement's main proponent. Historians compare the Quality Punk period to the Enlightenment movement of the 19th century.

Corporate accountability inches forward

After two high-profile catastrophes in 2018 and 2020, legislation regulates all companies to maintain 100-percent transparency. A new management school of business ethics honors the first graduating class of 2022, all proud recipients of an MBA in "doing business the right way."

And my most radical prediction for 2022: Management finally attunes its ears to the voice of the customer.

Honestly, I don't know what the future will bring, and I doubt my ideas warrant my joining the ranks of futurologists. However, I *can* confidently predict that our future will be full of the repeat mistakes and failures from our past. So when it comes time for your next strategic planning session, perhaps you could consider focusing less on the desired outcomes and more on the process of creating outcomes. I know in my 10-year plan, I will allow for the flexibility of change outside of my control.

Man Cave Manufacturing

Turning inspiration and ingenuity into quality training

My cell phone was vibrating like a dryer set at hyper-speed, and my wife's name popped up on the screen. My first thought was that something had gone wrong. I did tell her to call only if there were problems with the movers. I was on the other side of town, a prisoner at the Department of Motor Vehicles, waiting for my turn to be seen.

There wasn't much I could do if there was a problem, but I took her call anyway. "The removal guys are asking what a shed is," she said, laughing. To date, that is the oddest statement my wife has made during our monumental move from Scotland to America.

One of the many boxes in our sea freight that had just arrived had "shed tools" written in indelible ink on at least two sides. This was put on by the packers at the Scottish end, trying to help their American counterparts by directing them where the box should go. Although I found it hard to believe, the team of movers in Louisiana apparently had no terms of reference for "shed." Surely the word was one of the first that humans coined after they invented the wheel? Or maybe before they invented it, since sheds are where so many things get cobbled together.

In any case, I knew the "shed tools" were actually something else, and I was happy that the box had arrived. It meant that I would be able to release my shed projects on my new American colleagues, very soon. The shed tools were games I'd made to help co-workers understand quality principles. They were the results of many hours spent in the shed—or "man cave," as my wife calls it.

A word about UK shed culture is in order here. I suspect our terrible weather drives a great many people to spend hours fettling, making, and practicing their art forms indoors. On a typical rainy Saturday or Sunday, you'll find men in drafty, cold, wet, and moldy little wooden structures, with a dim light illuminating them at their hobbies. I, too, had my own little shed thing for a time. In fact, I had two sheds, both used in the highly efficient manufacture of my quality training games.

Sometimes I like to take people out of their comfort zones to get them to think about something differently. And after working with grown men who acted like children most of the time, it occurred to me that playing games at work might help me influence them faster. This was the motivating force behind my shed projects; the inspiration came from a training course where I was introduced to W. Edwards Deming's Red Bead Experiment. If you're unfamiliar with it, I implore you to read Henry R. Neave's account of it in chapter six of The Deming Dimension (Neave, 1990). The concept behind the experiment is that the "process"—white bead manufacturing—is contaminated with red beads.

Possessed by the idea of running this experiment at work, I was determined to get my hands on all the materials. I wondered whether it might have been turned into a children's board game, but I had no luck when I looked at the local toy warehouse store. Likewise I searched the Internet high and low without any success. However, I refused to abandon the idea. There was only one recourse left to me, and I took it: "To the man cave!" I cried, in the spirit of a 1960s caped crusader episode.

First I formulated my list: beads, lots of them; paddle with holes in it to pick up the beads; a big rectangular tub to hold everything. Although there was an excellent crafts supplier in my town, it turned out they didn't stock red beads. So I settled for black and white ones, since the principle was the same.

Next, the tub: I headed to IKEA, and it didn't take me long to find tubs in almost limitless sizes. I did get some strange looks from other customers when I emptied my large bag of beads into the different options, looking for the most suitable size.

The paddle was next. I knew I would have to fabricate this, but I hadn't considered how or with what. I sat in my kitchen having a cup of coffee, looking out the window at the shed. The fact that I didn't have the last necessary element perturbed me. How could I make this paddle? As I set my coffee cup down, still hot, onto the chopping board in the kitchen, the solution presented itself. My wife still hasn't forgiven me for absconding with that chopping board, although I do have a very elegant paddle as a result.

That was the first quality training game I made. I have since made three more; each designed to get a different message across, and all produced in my little wooden shed.

Now that we're living in America, I no longer have a shed. However, we do have a very nice spare bedroom in our apartment—or rather; we *did* have a spare room. It now serves as my man cave.

Does a Corporate Social Responsibility Report Demonstrate Responsibility?

Let us not confuse output for outcome

Oh no, it's happened again! Why do I do this to myself time and again? Do I need to seek help, professional assistance of a psychological nature? I must stop doing this; it's is as if I don't have control over myself. It's a habit. No, it's not that; it's something different. Its worse, a disease like a virus or parasite in my brain: I can't stop thinking about quality in everything I see or do.

Today my wife found me looking at a document, and although I wasn't aware I was doing it, I was audibly growling—a literal *"grrrrh!"*—at the words and pictures on the glossy document in my hands. Sometimes I can't control my inner quality beast, and when it escapes, bystanders have two options: run fast or improve their process.

"So what has got you sounding like an angry squirrel this time?" my wife said. (Note to self: My inner quality beast must be a small animal.) What had come into my possession was a company annual financial report, along with a corporate social responsibility (CSR) report. Because I was a shareholder, this was the company's yearly gift to me for investing in my future benefit. In effect I'm betting that this company will perform through time.

What really is the purpose of a CSR report? As a customer, I've never asked for one from any supplier or store, but as a shareholder, I get one sent to me with the annual financial report. Therefore I should be happy I have this shiny CSR report in my paws, for the princely sum of free. However, I'm looking at the document and trying to figure out what value I'm supposed to be getting from it, and unconsciously I'm making a beastly noise as a result.

Does this CSR report genuinely reflect the truth about how socially responsible this company really is, and how environmentally conscious its actions make them? Well, the company published it along with the financial report, so therefore it must be honest, right? Or is it sugar-coated propaganda, simply a selection of little golden nuggets portraying how environmentally conscious the company would like to appear?

But here's what really got me roaring like a squirrel: The Company had mixed up "output" with "outcome."

Long ago, when I was first introduced to this concept by my mentor, I didn't think there was any difference. I was immature in my quality thinking, and my inner quality squirrel hadn't yet woken from hibernation. "In any process you will have an output, and aren't output or outcome the same thing, really?" I wondered.

My mentor, who believed in the Socratic Method, asked in return, "Well, in a broken process, what would be the output? Is it the same as a desired outcome?" How frustrating for an immature quality professional. There I was, looking for an answer and being posed a new question. I was being coached subtly by a Master Quality Ninja, and I hadn't yet recognized it.

In a process you can have many inputs that are transformed into an output. This is my textbook definition of a process that I'd throw at Mr. Manager time and again. However, in common-man-speak, my definition is, "How we do things around here, using stuff that our suppliers give us, to provide a product or service to our customer."

Now if a process is broken, or one of the inputs has so much inherent variation that the process can't transform it effectively, the result is an output that could be classed as "nonconforming to requirements," which is an outcome. So I learned a valuable lesson: An output will not be the same as an outcome, and it's the outcome that we aim for in business, an outcome that can only be produced by our processes and process inputs.

So if I confuse an output (such as the CSR report I was reading) for an outcome (the company is environmentally sound and intertwined with the community), I quickly run into trouble. Please take my word for it: The Company's output and outcome are virtual strangers.

With instant media and Internet sources for information, we can easily see both sides to any tale. I can access the Environmental Protection Agency or government websites that publish prosecutions and fines this company has incurred. I can access social networking websites run by "hate" groups against this company. I can access video files of news reports showing a raging local, aggrieved by the company's action or inaction to the pollution it has caused.

All these points of information help me get a better understanding of the company's true nature. I can cross-reference the CSR report and see if any penalties or disgruntled groups pop up. None of which I can find—in fact, I can't even see the penalties in the financial report. Well done, accountants. You've probably delayed these massive payments until next year's financial report, painting a positive picture to encourage shareholders to invest further.

OK, so I've invested my money, and I have to accept that it really is like gambling, hoping to get a return somewhere down the line. As a quality professional, I understand that some companies, which are focused on the short term, do not succeed in the long run. It only took the first recession of this new century to wipe out many of these companies. Looking at the CSR report vs. the information online, I get a clear picture that perhaps the company's management is focused only on the bottom line rather than long-term sustainability. This helps me make an informed choice: thank you and good-bye.

I've had the privilege to hear and work with a great many "systems thinkers," learning that taking a systems approach can help everyone understand their company better. When taking this approach, perhaps we should consider our stakeholders in a different way. I've learned the hard way to recognize who my stakeholders are: They are the people who, when I haven't involved them in something, come at me holding a stake to drive through my heart.

As for the CSR report, I suspect there were many good intentions behind writing it for the stakeholders. But taking a systems-thinking perspective, who should we really ask to write the report? What would be the impact if perhaps an environmental agency wrote a critique? Or what would be the outcome if a "hate" campaigner was allowed to reply in the report? If companies want to be more transparent, then explaining the things that hurt their reputations, and describing how they are planning to put it right, would be of benefit to me, a stakeholder. Being honest enough to admit a mistake and, most important, taking action to prevent a recurrence, would be one step toward social responsibility. A CSR report will never do this; only management action will.

Returning to my roaring like a small mammal and the reasons why: The company declared how much paper it recycled in one year—thousands of tons of the stuff. But for some reason, the company still chose to print off thousands of copies of the CSR report on paper that never declared if it was recycled. Today I'll do my part for the environment:

The CSR report is now in the process of being turned into toilet paper, a much more value-added item.

Taking on Big Tabasco

Or, a little undercover research into le petit baton rouge

Recently I visited the world-famous Tabasco sauce factory on Avery Island, Louisiana. We live approximately 30 miles from the global super-brand, and what else would a quality professional like to do on his holiday downtime than visit a factory to see what lessons he could learn? And my wife believed she'd be going on a nice day trip... well, I did, for sure.

I like factory tours because they allow me to gain insight into other industries, their practices and techniques, and how they establish and promote quality. Since I am a Quality Ninja, skilled in stealthy sneakiness in my approach to gleaning information, I also use tours as an opportunity to learn how the business comes up with its solutions. Normally it's the process for creating solutions that stimulates me, not so much the solution. In the case of our Tabasco visit, this involved wondering how they came up with their solution to a quality need: How did they come up with their *petit baton rouge*, or "little red stick?"

Located on the banks of the Mississippi, Baton Rouge is the state capitol of Louisiana. Today this city is noted for its hugely successful college football team, the LSU Tigers. (Why is it called "football," when the ball is kicked only a handful of times?) From what I have been able to glean, the city was named when French explorers were ascending the river and came across the Native American territorial practice of lining the riverbanks with bloody stakes—hence, the French term for red stick: *baton rouge*. However, it wasn't the place Baton Rouge that caught my quality eye; it was *le petit baton rouge*, or the little red stick found in the Tabasco sauce factory near the city.

Anyway, as factory tours go, this one was very informative. I learned that her majesty Queen Elizabeth II enjoys a bit of the hot stuff and the factory gate has her royal seal of approval hanging above it. I learned that Tabasco sauce is exported to more than 180 countries, and each bottle is produced in this tiny enclave in Louisiana. Disappointingly, they weren't bottling or manufacturing on the Friday we were there, not due to a holiday but because they are so efficient, they only manufacture Monday through Thursday.

So we've got efficiency, customer feedback by way of royal decree, and a global super-brand all housed in a little red brick building no bigger than my apartment block.

But to return to the most brilliantly simple quality principle I picked up that day. As we watched a well-produced and informative video on the hard-working farmers who cultivate the peppers in South and Central America, it was proclaimed that "only an expert can tell a perfectly ripe pepper." So to help these pepper pickers produce the perfectly prepared and ripe peppers, they are issued a little stick, painted the very specific red, ripe pepper color. (If you wish to have more alliteration of "P" words, I would recommend meeting the tour guide at the factory. I think I counted her speaking 10 in a row in one sentence.) The little red stick is available for customers at the gift shop, along with other Tabasco merchandise.

What I really liked about this was how simple a quality idea it is. To me, Tabasco sauce is universally accepted, and I have seen it everywhere around the world. But I'd never really thought about how the company maintained the consistency that other mega-brands have. A glance at the side of the hot sauce bottle tells me there are few ingredients: peppers, vinegar, and salt. Since the key ingredient are the peppers for the spiciness and color, maintaining the consistency of the peppers themselves would be vital. However, anything that grows out of the ground, dependent on weather, soil, rain, and sunlight, is subject to wonderful variation, and in this case, the variation would be too difficult to reduce or eliminate.

Reducing variation in the pepper selection is undoubtedly an excellent outcome from having a comparator in the form of *le petit baton rouge*. It also reduces waste. Because the peppers are hand-picked, there is no discarding of under-ripe peppers; they are left on the plant to mature for the next day of picking. The need for training on selecting the perfect pepper is negated or very minimal, I would presume.

Tabasco's environmental credentials don't stop there: The Company also uses old barrels recycled from the Jack Daniels distillery. These are used in the process of turning the pepper mash into a sauce during a three-year period. To top it all, the factory grounds are located on an island nature reserve and bird sanctuary.

So how did Tabasco achieve excellence and consistency? Was it by a super Six Sigma Master Black Belt? Was it a world expert in quality improvement? Well, no. It was a small business that found a creative solution to a problem that it took the time to understand. It was a business that deemed the quality of its product the most important element, and it created a solution that also helps stakeholders outside its factory gates.

This is a similar story to other great companies, but there's one difference that sets this company apart from Toyota, Apple, or Google: The McIlhenny family has been able to sustain the vision of Edmund McIlhenny's Tabasco sauce business since the 1880s. I laugh at myself for not recognizing this sooner. A pupil of the Toyota principle for so long, I failed to see quality in a different industry. Yet that little bottle with its bright red top has been a part of my life for as long as I can remember, either in a cupboard or on a table, as consistent as the Earth spinning on its axis, as reliable as a wood-burning stove, and instantly recognizable as a... well, as a bottle of Tabasco sauce.

Sometimes it's difficult to recognize quality when you're so familiar and accustomed to your own version of it. I would suggest it's the same for you as it is for me. Perhaps it's time we bring an outsider, maybe a customer, to our businesses to help us recognize our business qualities or our personal qualities. Let's take that opportunity not to highlight our successes, as nice as they are, but to remind ourselves of how we got there. Ask what was the process that led us to quality? What was the driver for us to achieve it, and do we still have what it takes to get us there again?

My day trip to a little factory inspired me to get an outsider to look at my business. This week I'm asking three outsiders to visit me: an overseas colleague, a supplier, and a customer. To each one I will be posing the same question: What qualities do you see? This will help me start to understand what, where, and how we achieved these qualities in the past. It will be a starting point for creating quality or updating my processes, for sustaining and improving our quality achievements.

I love my work in quality. In what other role could you have such a wonderful opportunity to promote growth, all from a little red stick seen on a day trip?

Which Standard Will You Select?

Accreditation doesn't guarantee quality in an organization

The menu has folded out into four sections. Each page has a picture next to the delicious option; however, I know the server will be taking the menu away from me after I've placed my order. I'm pondering how I can confirm that my order is the same as the picture. Perhaps I should ask if they have a quality system in place to guarantee satisfaction.

What other elements of this restaurant am I relying on? Does the kitchen clean its surfaces per the hygiene code? Is the refrigerator's temperature set as recommended by the FDA to reduce the risk of bacterial growth? Has the food been sourced from ethically and environmentally conscious sources? Here comes the server. I'll take the opportunity to ask him a clarifying question or two.

"Excuse me, could you possibly enlighten me on something?"

"Sure can, sir, how can I help?" says the young man with terribly fashionable and precisely shaped facial hair.

"I'm wondering if you could tell me if your restaurant has ISO 9001 certification."

Before finishing my sentence, an explosion of pain and adrenaline pulsates in my shin. Fighting the heartbeat of nausea, I see a look of confusion on the server's face and anger in my wife's eyes. I realize two things at that moment: Mentioning ISO 9001 could be meaningless to non-quality folks, and my wife has the accuracy of an NFL kicker to precisely and powerfully put her shoe through my leg. I've embarrassed her again by letting my inner quality beast loose at an inappropriate time.

I'll start off by saying I'm not a fan of ISO 9001. I've probably limited my career by stating this, but when you explain ISO 9001 to a non-quality professional; do you experience the dead-in-the-eyes look? The issue for me is not what the standard's original intent was or what its initiators were trying to achieve, which I think is honorable and admirable. My problem concerns what the standard has turned industry into.

If you're unfamiliar with ISO 9001, it is essentially a specification, developed with contributions from countries from all over the world. The International Organization for Standardization (ISO), located in Geneva, is a collaborative bunch of people who set out guidelines for commonality and standardization for our modern global economy. Without ISO, many of the items in your home or business wouldn't exist, so I'm grateful for ISO's work.

ISO 9001 is only one of the many standards in the ISO library, but this document scopes out the minimum expectations for a "system" that can provide some level of quality for an organization. I've used the word "minimum" for a reason. If your company becomes certified to ISO 9001, it doesn't necessarily mean it instantly becomes a quality company. Having a certified quality system is no guarantee that problems go away, although there are some people who believe that's true. This is where my ISO 9001 problems start: confusing certification to a quality system standard as a mark of guaranteed quality.

Due to this confusion, we have customers telling their supply chains they must be ISO 9001-certified. They must be on an approved list. We have certification auditors granted with powers that make Lord Voldemort look like a weakling. We have companies going through the motions of achieving certification, and consequently gaining nothing more than a shiny, hologrammed memento, presented in a cheap plastic frame at a reception.

If the idea was to standardize, through ISO 9001, the best practices of quality organizations worldwide, then I'm all for it. I like standardization. I like to be a satisfied customer. However, ISO 9001 certification can cause so many odd repercussions that my belief in its ability to standardize for a common vision has eroded. I know this viewpoint will not win many over, but I'd like to consider some alternate standards or specifications that could also help companies achieve quality. Where should we start looking? My recommendations are as follows, and they are in no particular order:

The law. This is a vast area and also the quickest route to shut down your business, should you fall on the wrong side of the law. The challenge in complying with legal requirements is in their interpretation. Beyond interpretation, the dilemma is which law to prioritize first. I would say if there are any moral concerns within your business about employees, the environment, or the community, then legislation that addresses these topics would be a good hunting ground. For example, health and safety laws are there for a reason, and if the data in your business show you're hurting your employees, you can expect a visit from a governmental health and safety inspector, along with a fine on your financial manager's desk.

Your customer. Sometimes your customer will help you by providing detailed expectations. These might be engineering drawings or requirements listed on the purchase request. At other times your customer could be ignorant about your requirements. Therefore, taking a step closer to your customer to ask for clarifications may help. You might have to develop an understanding of their requirements in your company's language. I like to use the critical to quality characteristics (CTQC) technique. I've used this in the past to get a much better understanding of customer requirements. World-class companies use this a great deal to stimulate continuous improvement and innovation, and to overcome the problems of why they are not achieving customer requirements.

Your suppliers. You have selected these groups of people to support you with products or services because they are probably experts in their fields. Perhaps you can get something from them—a better understanding of your standards or of the specialty area they are in. Recently I facilitated a workshop with a supplier and received the feedback that my supplier wanted to understand why certain features on our engineering drawing had such tight tolerance. Not an unusual request, but as a customer, we never put into context for the supplier why we ask for that tolerance. Explaining that it went into an assembly and the feature was critical in the performance of the device helped the supplier understand why the part is designed that way. As a result, we all took actions to define new standards so we can work together better in the future.

Industry codes. In every industry I've worked in, I have come across numerous codes. These can be a collection of best practices, lessons learned, or a formal requirement that has evolved to support compliance with a legal framework. In many ways, industry codes are a collection of best practices from very complex processes. I like these because they tend to be written in the language of the industry. Sometimes they eventually become international standards, absorbed into the ISO family or some other system.

Awards and competitions. Not all of these will help improve quality. Many awards are superficial and require at most completing a form and submitting evidence. However, the better awards that require your business to be checked by an outside party, someone who will take a thorough and detailed look at your performance, will help. Learning from failing to win an award is a useful step in the process of continuous improvement. The Baldrige Award is a process, not just an award application that each contestant goes through. Simply going through the Baldrige program has been beneficial to many companies. If I had the choice, I'd rather go for a supplier that has won the Deming Medal or Shingo Prize over a supplier that is ISO 9001-certified.

Your business. Within any business there's always the "way things are done around here." But how are we to define this? Have you ever wondered why one operator may produce better products than another? A brilliant statistician I learned from many years ago once told me about a tire factory he worked in. The factory produced retreaded tires and through analysis discovered that one operator produced less variation. They studied what he did and wrote down "his" favored settings on the machine he operated. They did this with the idea of using the same settings across the factory, defined in a standardized procedure. When they tried this out, they found that variation actually increased. After further investigation, they discovered that the control knob was broken on the star operator's machine, so whatever setting he dialed made no difference. The factory then standardized the machines: less variation resulted in better tires. I like defining standards in your own business. It's comparatively easy, everything you need to do is at your disposal, and you get tremendous gains from doing this, much more than if your objective is to become ISO 9001-certified.

Your competitors. This may seem like a mad idea, but research and development of new technology can often outpace the development of standards in your industry. But by working in collaboration with your peers, you have an opportunity to share resources and develop common standards for mutual benefit.

International standards. Well, I've already weighed in about ISO 9001. What I prefer to do with this category is speak to the people behind the standards. These folks are often a great source of knowledge because they tend to be experts in their fields, and they can usually express the concepts in a language anyone can understand.

Let us always set our standards high. If our current standards are easy to achieve, then we must question if they are really worth it. My personal philosophy is that everything is broken or wrong: Even if something is good today, I want to do my best to improve it tomorrow. This is the only standard I have.

If you're reading this in the office, I ask you to stand up, open your office door, and shout out to your colleagues, "Our standards are failing us!" See what reactions you get. Assuming you aren't hauled off by human resources for doing this, start talking to your colleagues about what your company needs to do to raise the bar.

Finally, please give me feedback about this article. You've taken the time to consider my writing, and I need your help to raise my standards. If you know of an ISO writing standard, please tell me. My man-cave wall is bare of hologrammed accreditation certificates.

Résumé Help

Ten tips to land your dream job

The pile of papers in front of me is sizable. I'm wondering what would be the correct term for the volume of these white sheets of paper. A group of lions is called a "pride"; is a group of résumés called a "wedge," a "stack," or a "flurry?" I'm distracting myself from the reality of having to work my way through each snowy page, now covering my desk like a blizzard.

I have a fluorescent highlighter in my left hand and a red pen in my right. If a photograph were taken of me at this instant, I would appear to be taking an if-you-can-eat-this-Texas-sized-steak-you-eat-for-free challenge. However, my steak is bigger than Texas. It is so big, I fear it. And my challenge is to review all of these résumés in front of me.

How can I fear documents? I'm a quality professional, and I'm very used, or at least conditioned, to reviewing poorly written documents. Why am I dreading looking at résumés? I suppose with corporate documentation, procedures can be discussed with the author or reviewed with the team involved in the process. But it's unlikely I'll meet with résumé authors, and therefore I've got a whole lot of thinking to do.

The reason for bringing this up with you, my quality sisters and brothers, is so I can share my observations and help if you're out there, unemployed. I want to help arm you against your competition, the competition that's after that dream job of yours.

The Internet abounds with advice, so why should you bother to let a gobshite quality professional give you his 10 cents? Perhaps, as a quality professional, I'm in a better position to give advice in our field of expertise. During the last few years, the topsy-turvy economy has bestowed several opportunities for me to help others prepare their résumés. I don't remember really how I was asked; however, I've helped dozens of neighbors and friends fine-tune their résumés or find a new career path. And many have been invited to the interview stage, all as a result of some guidance I've provided. I remember helping a friend out, and when he showed his résumé to his wife, she said, "You're damn sexy on paper," a different response from what I'd imagined.

Here are a few of my favorite hints and tips for résumés: **Acronyms or initials.** If the help-wanted ad looks as if Scrabble tiles have fallen on the page, don't assume that the person who wrote the ad has any idea what the acronyms mean. This also applies to your résumé. If you have a résumé that reads like alphabet spaghetti, and you don't include the meanings or context, your résumé will appear in my T-file. T is for trash.

Quantity does not mean quality. Now in my business, if an operator is faced with a procedure that's more than three pages long, they are likely not to implement it because it's too complex to follow. As a quality professional in this situation, you would confer with the operator and simplify the procedure. What do you think would happen if you submitted a 10-page résumé to me? I'm a busy guy, and I don't have the patience to go through more than three pages.

No pictures, please. I live in the real world, and I know that people will embellish (that is UK politeness for barefaced lie) their résumé. If you enclose a picture of Brad Pitt and expect me to think it's you, good luck to you, my friend. I'm a quality professional, not a casting agent; therefore, I'm interested in your skills, not your looks.

Apply quality control. What good documentation practices have you seen in your career (e.g., page numbering, document reference heading on each page)? Why not put your name on each page at the top? It will only help the reviewer.

Read the job advertisement. Surprisingly, many people think that a generic résumé will apply for all situations. Every job listing has key words or phrases to convey its message to the right candidate. If you don't have the necessary skills defined in the ad, then think of your transferrable skills.

Make it professional, not fancy. Don't bother with colored paper, colorful banners, or artistic text unless you are going to apply for a "creative" company. Even then, if you are applying to a creative business, colored paper wouldn't constitute showing flare or imagination.

Electronic documentation best practices. I suggest you save and share your résumé as a PDF file. The number of e-mailed files that I've received in Microsoft Word format that display edit notes and change history, and open with auto spell check highlighting errors, is beyond belief.

Get someone not involved in quality to review your résumé. Keep in mind that someone other than a quality professional may look over your résumé in the organization to which you are applying. Find a friend who can proofread, and welcome their suggestions or requests for clarification of what you've written. This can be helpful to improve your résumé.

Keep it up to date. If you are thinking about sending in a job application, it would be prudent to review your résumé, which will be going with it. You don't want a résumé years out of date going to a potential employer.

Explain gaps in your career history. If you were unemployed for a variety of reasons, explain those reasons and be succinct. Otherwise, the reader's imagination may fill the gap with a prison sentence for murdering your last boss. And if that was truly the case, I suggest leaving out the reason you were incarcerated.

Good hunting, my friend. If you take my advice, if it works for you and you get the job of your dreams, remember me, please. Especially if you see me at the end of the bar, looking thirsty. And if you do, please note that I only drink champagne, by the pint.

The Best Investigation Technique

Part of our job is teaching others to solve quality issues by consensus

During the mid-1980s, two great schools of investigation were put up against each other. Each was immensely popular, and still is today, with fans firmly seated in one methodology or the other. One school was led by a disheveled, cigar-smoking character. The other had a lady more akin to your favorite, mild-mannered auntie at the helm. Both fought for the No. 1 spot.

I can see them in my mind's eye, duking it out. The scene is Madison Square Garden, complete with overexcited commentators:

"Ladies and gentlemen, welcome to Madison Square Garden. I'm Ken Bhan, your commentator tonight. With me ringside is Jed Okra."

"Thanks, Ken. What a magnificent setting for this slightly different martial arts event."

"That's right, Jed. In just a moment we'll be seeing two warriors, two mighty names in the business, duking it out."

At this point I imagine the lights dimming. I hear the crowd chanting and loud music blaring. The gladiators, fighting for the honor of their investigative techniques, are walking to the center of the ring. And there's Bruce Buffer waiting to meet them and announce the fight.

"Ladies and gentlemen, boys and girls, let's get ready to RUMBLLLLLLLLLLLLLE!"

The crowds erupt. In the distance, I hear the muffled ring of a telephone.

"In the blue corner," continues Buffer as the crowd settles down, "fighting from the West Coast, from Los Angeleeeese, is your how-do-you-catch 'em champion, Lieutenant Columboooo!"

The crowd grows frantic, cheering and shouting. I hear some elements booing. And that phone is still ringing.

"And in the red corner, long-time author and advocate of the whodunit, Jessicaaaaaa Fletcher!"

"What a crowd, Ken, Have you ever heard such a cheer?"

"The waiting is over now, Jed, it's *Columbo* vs. *Murder She Wrote,* and I can't wait to see which prevails."

The starting bell sounds.

"Look at Columbo, straight at Jessica like a punishing kangaroo. He's hit her with a surprise left hook!"

"That's got to hurt, Ken. I think a low-flying tooth just missed me."

The ringing of the phone is now louder than ever.

"Ooooh, Jed, what a comeback! That little lady just put her knee through his...."

"Ken, Columbo is down! Ouch, that would make any grown man cry."

"My advice, Jed, is not to hold them but to count them!"

The ringing phone has snapped me out of my daydream. I'm back in a Saturday morning, in my man cave, also known as the office in my apartment. The computer screen shows the face of an old quality friend from Scotland, trying to reach me via Skype.

"Afternoon, Paul…."

I've always been bit of a daydreamer. That morning I'd been preparing for my friend's call. He'd recently changed employers, to a small but fast-growing business. He's perfect for this company; his tenacity and passion will help mature the business. However, he's always looking to get a second opinion on his thoughts before taking any action. I'd received an e-mail from him earlier in the week. It arrived after 6 p.m. from Scotland, which is six hours ahead, so that meant my friend was in dire need of help. Due to the company's multiple quality issues and his recent arrival as the quality assurance manager, two of the company's customers had pounced on him.

His business is a small engineering company that services a handful of customers—a complete opposite of where my friend and I had trained and worked together. Recent audits had highlighted the need for the business to adopt and investigation techniques to improve the quality of what the supplier was receiving. (Why is it necessary, if your supplier has quality issues, to first resort to an audit?)

What I'd gathered from the e-mail was that the two customers were recommending two different, branded, investigation techniques. One was a variation of 5 Whys, the other a method of cause-and-effect analysis. Going forward, each customer wanted its technique to be used when dealing with future quality issues. I did some research on these techniques and reviewed the books in my quality library (when I say "library," I mean the shelves my wife has designated as "the boring business books") to prepare some ideas to share with my friend.

Collecting my thoughts before the call, my imagination had wandered into the weird, enchanted forest in my head, where I conjured Columbo fighting with Jessica Fletcher. I guess I was visualizing the two different customers' preferred techniques, and trying to decide which would be the better methodology. I like to visualize my challenges. I often ride the unicorn of improvement, at a galloping pace, through my place of work.

Anyway, we considered the pros and the cons of each of his customer's techniques. We noted how each technique originated from the same core ideas. We talked about our own approaches and philosophies from our favorite quality thinkers. We concluded that his company already had a defined investigation process, which wasn't working at that point in time.

A caring customer had audited the business and discovered that his company wasn't following the customer's own processes. Consequently, it was recommended to use a different approach, which from the customers' perspective was quite effective. Repeated problems had escalated the issue, and the customer wanted to be part of future investigations. So why shouldn't the customer recommend its preferred systems? The challenge my friend had was that a second auditor made a similar recommendation—i.e., change the investigation methodology. My friend's boss, who was also joint owner of the company, instructed him to adopt both techniques, and it had to be done yesterday.

What my friend didn't realize was that I was double-, or rather, triple-teaming him with Lt. Columbo and Jessica Fletcher subtly helping the investigation. I think I even unleashed the question, "Just one more thing...."

My friend's business was going through some very uncomfortable growing pains. Due to rapid growth and the niche that his new employer had created, issues were being investigated. However, due to limited resources, the team at his new workplace didn't have adequate "time" or "coaching" to test and verify the effectiveness of the actions. In essence it was the immediate, rather than the true root cause that was being addressed.

Of course, he knew this already. I think he just wanted someone to ask logical questions to test his ideas. He has been conditioned to think like this from when we worked together in a much larger and mature organization.

The issue wasn't really his boss asking him to choose one technique over another, and it wasn't the customer trying to flex some powerful muscle. It was his inexperience in recognizing that there was a need to mentor the organization's leadership in solving quality issues by consensus. He and I are fortunate in our past; the leaders at our previous company would seriously and proactively address issues. This was the first time he realized his role and importance in developing the quality culture at his new workplace.

I imagine our next call will be about the cultural changes on the path to excellence he's now initiated. And I expect my imagination will take me beforehand to distant realms, fighting armies of saber-toothed squirrels with W. Edwards Deming and Bruce Lee by my side.

A Week in the Life of a Sales Professional

We quality types must also be adept at selling difficult and strange ideas

Sales professionals, according to some circles at least, aren't all that different from us quality professionals. I once believed they were two-faced liars, because they'd sell their mother to get that precious sales commission. However, as a systems thinker, I like to get my facts straight before drawing conclusions. I'm sure you do, too.

The following is an excerpt from the week of a typical sales professional. It's built from my collection of conversations with a mystery sales professional—who shall remain anonymous—and as such is written in the first person.

Sunday. With the knowledge of the meeting tomorrow with the sales and marketing manager, operations manager, and vice president, I have to prepare the presentation. A PowerPoint masterpiece, with analysis of past performance and future opportunities. I must break down the different product groups and target opportunities... that would easily give me more slides.

Spreadsheets are open in multiple windows on my screen. Data are being pulled from the costs tab, the profits tab, and the customers tab. I select rows upon rows of these little white boxes; the little black dollar signs are being copied and pasted. I've created a bar chart. I have inner turmoil: Do I choose 2-D or 3-D bars? I figure 2-D is better; however, I must color-code the bars to the VP's favorite sports team. (Who puts mustard yellow and pink together as a uniform?) Regardless, these are the colors I must use to win him over.

Realizing that the time will be short to convey my big message, I must also keep the presentation short and to the point. I've trimmed it down from 67 slides to 64.

Monday. Meeting is at 11 a.m. My shoes are clean, USB pen in my pocket with the presentation; I am prepared. It's going to be great. I need to sell my ideas to the VP and clinch that sale. It's now my turn to make it big, and for the senior people in the business to remember my name.

I give the presentation. I'm flawless in my delivery. Questions are posed, I respond immediately, and where I can't answer, I don't lie or hide that I don't know some answers. They would easily see past that sham, so I need to stick at what I am here to do: sell.

I can't read the room after the delivery. It's like a world poker-face tournament. Have I won them over? Have I made the sale? The sales manager jots a note. The VP glances at his watch. The second hand on the clock is the only sound I hear; do I break the silence? No, I'll let them fill the silent void. "You've got it," declares the VP. He confers with the sales manager and agrees on a target for this opportunity. "Your target will be 10 percent higher than the projections," he says. He gets up and leaves.

I did it. I figure that it must have been the chart colors that sealed the deal. I celebrate with a 30-minute lunch break, but then it's back to work.

Tuesday. My day starts early; the alarm calls me awake at 5 a.m. My first thought is to make that winning pitch today to the actual customer. By 6:30 I'm waiting in a coffee shop ordering nearly $50 of mixed doughnuts and pints of coffee. This is my route into my external customer's world, the people paying for our services. The plan is that by arriving early, I can use these treats to get the full attention of some key players at my customer's office.

I get there with my boxes and tray of delights. I find that the door swings wide open for me, and I'm in. There's no getting rid of me now. I make small talk with some tediously dull man, who can't get my name right. That, I don't have issue with; however, come on, dude, I bring you coffee and doughnuts, and you can't find the courtesy to say, "Thank you?" I will take a moment later during my drive home to think of ways I could make that coffee taste unpleasant.

I now see the project manager for our ongoing project walking through the corridor. She sees me. A scowl at first recognition. I'm going to change that to a smile and get her to agree with what I'm about to say. "Hey good morning... and before you ask me to leave, I'll trade you a latte for 10 minutes of your time." I've got her full attention now.

We talk at length. I pitch my idea to her, this time without a PowerPoint. She is the type of person who doesn't work with slick presentations. I think that she responds better to an emotional state of mind. It is a win-win proposal I'm making, and I am sharing a future image of mutual benefit. Layering it on thick with "how things will be," I tell her how the proposal will make her project easier. She buys the idea, and I get the work as a result. She asks me to send her the "numbers" over by email, for review later.

I call the sales manager with the news. He congratulates me, then as a reward, lets me know that I'm playing golf on Friday.

Wednesday. Knowing that the operations department will soon be posed with a new challenge from the customer, I need to relay my news to them. Operations, I know, are a bigger challenge to influence. The volume of work with clients is currently high, and making a change may be as welcome as a fart in a submarine. I must work hard at making this a sell to the operations manager.

The operations manager takes it well. In essence I've told him that we've got a new opportunity, and he's going to have to make some inward investment. However, when I told him that the customer will pay for that investment, he was receptive to the notion. I think I've now tallied three sales this week, with 100-percent achievement.

Called the sales manager, tried to move the Friday golf to today. He said no.

Thursday. Negotiation training has been on my training list for some time, and it's today. A slick outfit of consultants are preparing for the day with a stack of papers in the corner. I'm one of 12 in the room, part of a mix of supply-chain professionals, operation managers, and sales. The consultants start off with an ice-breaker in mini-groups of three, and I'm teamed up with the office deviant and the only girl from supply chain. We had to "draw" an interesting fact about each other. With my group, it felt more like protecting the U.S. president than breaking the ice.

The trainers then handed out an assessment, and 30 questions later we draw a chart with our "negotiation profile." One of the trainers looks down at my chart and comments, "It's almost a perfect match to the ideal negotiation profile." Any small ego boost for a Thursday is very welcome.

The training runs through a variety of scenarios, some role-playing and group exercises. The team I'm in comes out on top each time. I found that I've gotten more out of the training that I thought I would, and a better understanding of the people I work alongside.

Friday. Golfing today or specifically, this afternoon. I start the morning reviewing the marketing materials and all the many emails I've missed while I was out training. The tee time arrives quickly, and I'm ready to play. I purposely pull some shots and allow the customer to beat me.

Saturday. It has been a long week, and I need my weekend off to rest. However, my wife has greater plans for my time, revolving around her assertion, "I need to go to the mall." I assume my traditional role, that of chief bag carrier. There, in the poorly lit building, being led around each identical store, I'm embarrassed by the other sales professionals. Being asked, "Is there anything I can help you with?" in a store where only 18-year-olds would be able to fit into the clothes. I've hit the point in my life where elastic features are a selling point for my pants selection. I couldn't stop myself and had to respond to that question with, "Kid, let me teach you a better question. One that may help you make your personal targets for today." But at that point my wife overheard my intervention and made at me with a coat hanger. "Can you please stop improving quality?" she groused. "It's your day off."

By now you readers will have realized that the week in a sales professional's life I've just described was my week. In quality we must be adept at selling difficult and strange ideas. Many of the skills I've learned the hard way came about due to the way I approached an influencing opportunity. My skills are no different than a sales professional's: I need to convey an idea, I need to build business cases, I need to meet and entertain customers. I need to sell quality every day; otherwise, we will stop moving forward.

Influencing is the art of selling, and although I would not recommend getting hung up on job titles, if you work in quality, you also may have to consider yourself a sales professional. You're selling the art of doing things better. If you're considering your training plans for next year, why not think about attending any sales training that is available? Like me, you may learn better ways to speak to someone, and get them to buy your quality ideas.

My Toyota Dilemma, Part Two

Field notes on car-purchasing, American style

I wrote a piece titled "My Toyota Dilemma," what I considered a nice little story about how I, an avid fan of the Toyota quality principles, didn't actually own a Toyota, and how ironic that was. However, *Quality* fans, I can now declare that I am—well, really my wife is—a proud owner of a Toyota automobile.

In the fall of 2011, I relocated, through my employer, from the United Kingdom to Louisiana. Moving to the United States meant we had to sell our European cars, but this wasn't due to the fact that the steering wheel is on the right side of the car (and when I say "right," I mean that it's on the correct side). We sold them because moving our cars wasn't part of the relocation package.

Once we arrived in Louisiana, my wife and I applied for Social Security numbers, and then we experienced being processed at the DMV. Having passed our driving tests, we were granted driver's licenses. Public transport isn't a ready solution for us where we now live, so I thought we could pick up a couple of cheap cars to get us from A to B.

As I've observed before, America in general is obsessed with cars. I have colleagues who have at least two cars for themselves: their commuter cars and their weekend cars. The weekend car in Louisiana tends to be a pickup because weekends are for driving the boat to the fishing grounds or transporting whatever has been hunted. I thought there would be a plentiful supply of low-mileage, inexpensive cars to choose from, as I would expect in the UK. However, this is where I found my first pitfall.

Let me explain the difference between the UK and U.S. car markets. Within the UK, the government has a set of policies that address European climate change targets. These policies range from heavily taxing polluting cars to setting higher taxes on fuel purchased. In addition to the environmental taxes, there are safety laws to abide, which require having your vehicle assessed in annual inspections. You rarely see pickup trucks or cars older than 10 years in the UK. With gasoline at nearly $10 per gallon, filling a 36-gallon tank in a pickup is an expensive experience at the pump. Factoring an average of 20 mpg around town, you'll have to plan your journey via the gas station. All this encourages the motorist to think of buying high-economy engines or fuels, which forces the "used" price of gas guzzlers down.

The annual inspection performed on vehicles (three years and older in the UK) also affects the pocketbook and used prices. Every year a government-approved station conducts a series of checks on safety features and engine emissions. And this safety check is linked to a national database, which is linked to the police force. So if your vehicle hasn't been assessed on time and with a passing score, your insurance is void and the UK police can remove the car from the road—even crush it into a cube if they're really in a bad mood. Your car's emissions are also linked to how much annual tax you must pay; so the less efficient the engine is, the more it costs you to drive.

Coming back to the pickup example, you might have to pay $800 per year for the environmental tax, and if you must also fix all the safety failures, then remedial annual repairs can get costly. Again, this all drives down the value of your used car.

So within the UK, you can readily find cars about 10 years old that cost less than $1,500; however, you may have to pay out more for inefficiency, work to correct any safety concerns, and pay higher tax duties. With America bursting at the seams with cars, I figured I'd be presented with the same "cheap" options. What a mistake that was.

In the UK, the annual inspection takes a least half a day: checking for tire wear, brake efficiency, corrosion, seat-belt integrity, engine emissions, light functions, leaks of any sort, wiper blade condition, windshield cracks, and many more too long to list—all for a $75 fee, even if you fail the inspections. If you do fail, you have a set period of time to correct and have your car re-inspected. If your car can't pass, and you choose to scrap it, you may have to pay the scrap merchant a disposal fee to take care of the environmentally dangerous parts lurking in your car. Where I live now, the annual inspection for vehicles consists of "if you can drive it to the inspection garage, you've passed," and it cost me $10 for the pleasure of a square sticker in my windshield.

With little to encourage the average car owner to keep the car to high standards, or government policies for driving (excuse the pun) environmental improvements in Louisiana, there's not much incentive to force down the cost for used vehicles. I do observe that brand new cars are much cheaper than their equivalents in the UK; however, the depreciation curve is much steeper in the UK on used cars.

Putting all this into a quality perspective, in the UK the senior leadership (i.e., the government) is trying to create a culture of efficiency by hitting the taxpayer where it hurts. As a result we have more cars on the road that are safer and also environmentally friendly. To illustrate the contrast between UK and Louisiana cars, I've included some examples of vehicles I'm fairly certain would never be allowed on UK roads.

Example 1: The non-opening side of the car. How would you be able to exit in an emergency? I personally appreciate the effort in the black panel stripe. Not so good is the paint on the replacement window.

Example 2: The lightweight model. Note the string holding the bumper on. This was taken when we were travelling on the interstate.

Example 3: The creative bumper solution using two by fours

Returning to the Toyota experience, my wife had done some great research at the local dealerships and identified another Japanese manufactured car online. So she went to see it, only to find that the dealer had sold it. However, they had just received a Toyota as a trade-in; she test drove it and liked it. So after work I went and looked at it myself. Given my experience with the UK system, having bought and owned many used cars in the UK, and knowing what to look for in a used car, to my mind I already had an advantage over the dealership.

Before taking the Toyota out for a spin, I was under the hood, on the floor under the car, checking the electrical system, feeling the viscosity of the oil, opening caps, and taking notes in my little notepad. The salesman was very adamant that this was an excellent "example" and kept reminding me that it was a trade-in. He threw out a value he was willing to sell it to me for, but with my list in hand, I fired back about the safety concerns I had (knowing there is a litigious culture in the U.S. can work to your advantage). We played this game for awhile until I got him to agree to fix many of the issues, at his cost, and a whacking great discount besides.

Since owning the Toyota, we have travelled all across Texas and Louisiana in it, and I absolutely enjoy every minute driving it. My wife recently asked me to upgrade the stereo to accept her iPod. Pulling the dash apart, I was exposed to a new element of the Toyota quality model: the hidden insides of the car. I was able to see the level of simplicity and mistake-proofing designed into the car. The dash components are so well made that that there are few screws or bolts. The snap-fit latches when reassembled and it's strong and fast. Thanks to the car's excellent design, even a bumbling idiot like me can ensure quality during the reassembly process.

So do I no longer have a Toyota dilemma now that I own one? Actually, I have a new Toyota dilemma. I live approximately 7 hours away from San Antonio. There is a mega Toyota factory there that builds pickup models. It is my intention to visit the factory and take a tour, and therein lies my dilemma: who to take with me. Do I take the managers who have never been exposed to a world-class production system? Do I take high-potential employees by way of a reward? Do I take the quality professionals to let them learn about the Toyota Production System? Do I do the tourist thing and take my wife for a nice day-trip, like I did to the Tabasco sauce factory? Or do I fill up a bus?

As with my previous Toyota dilemma, I will use the 5 Whys technique to help me out. It always gets me to where I should be.

The Art of Writing Procedures

How to become an artisan of quality

These days' quality professionals have shifted away from actually writing procedures to helping others develop documentation to describe the businesses they are in. Although I live in hope, I still see many poor attempts at "procedures"—or at least failures in their facilitation.

I have a simple view of the world: A management system's purpose is to describe how you do your business. Because customers and industry overseers will influence its design and content, you must be very strong to prevent an accreditation body from dictating what it should or should not contain.

Writing a quality management system (QMS) document truly is an art, an art in the medium of quality. As such, why do we allow non-artists to create such documents?

Perhaps my experiences will help you budding artists tasked with developing procedures, work instructions, or forms for your business. Traditionally, these documents live in something called a quality manual, which is part of a QMS.

So there you are with the building blocks of a management system, complete with all the documents within. Most likely you've inherited documents, and it's become your responsibility to "update" them. I don't like the word "update" in this instance. I prefer "correct" because there is often a great deal of correction needed in this world of ours.

Consider the words in your procedures. Were they written by anyone involved in the process they were designed to support? Unfortunately I've seen time and again a 40-page masterpiece an engineer has developed that is incomprehensible to anyone other than a superstar engineer. And the only person who will ever read this document will be a quality professional, and that will be during an audit. What a regretful waste of time and resources. Why not get the people who actually perform the process to document the way that they do things, and get an engineer to approve it if necessary? I've found that this way, process users take ownership of the procedures, with greater compliance to them as a natural result.

Because we live in a world connected by this thing called the Internet, you no doubt also have a global management system, where a colleague 12 time zones away has to comply with the company's complex instructions. Living and working in a country where English is the primary language, are we ignorant to the fact that English is the secondary or tertiary language for many of our colleagues overseas? Could there be something that is lost in translation?

Take for example South Africa, which recognizes 11 languages. English is spoken by 8 percent of the population: Should we translate? This reminds me of a recent discussion I had over which "English" will be used in procedures: American or British English (or as I like to call it, Americanese or Proper). Being from the UK, I speak and write in "Proper"; however, the team at Quality Digest likes to add the colored stains of Americanese to my columns and translate for you, dear reader. (Guys, did you just edit the "u" out of that "coloured" in the last sentence?)

Why would I think this is an unimportant discussion to have? If you need to describe how you do things around your business, just get it down on paper and worry about the spelling afterwards.

Back to my South Africa example, I believe we should work to ensure that any business information is expressed in a way that is meaningful to its stakeholders, and we should always consider translation. Otherwise I'd be fearful that an engineering instruction, containing important safety information but not translated into Xhosa, might put a colleague at risk in South Africa.

That brings me to another issue of quality management systems: how we access or grant access to the information. I will always strongly argue for having the information you need at the point of use—although the closest point many people have to this information is the computer that serves as the doorway to the Internet. It's worth considering that you share your documents via an intranet system. However, what are the computer literacy rates in your global business? Using the South African example again, where 4.2 percent (Gomez, 2010)of the population have access to computers, will your message get across?

I've explained that we need to translate to a language that is meaningful to the user, and that putting it online may not get to the intended user. However, I have not explained how to become an artisan of quality, or the art of writing procedures.

Being mindful that America does rank 10th for literacy in the world, there are some great examples of procedures that have been written in such a way that the user will get the engineer's instruction and it will be at the point of use for the user. And I want you, my dear quality professional, to see what a non-Americanese-speaking company has done to ensure that important instructions are communicated effectively: the instruction procedure for building an IKEA bookshelf. It is a perfect example of how to write a world-class procedure. Since it offers no guarantee of the user's abilities to ensure quality in the assembly process, I would recommend some level of adult supervision.

Granted, not all rules or requirements can be expressed visually, and you may have to consider your art of the procedure expressed in a different medium. For each document that you facilitate that describes your business, please be mindful of its intended customer or user, and how it will be available at its point of use. And most of all, "keep it simple, stupid" (KISS). All of which leads me to the parable of the CEO's procedures:

A fellow had just been hired as the new CEO of a large corporation. The CEO who was stepping down met with him privately and presented him with three procedures, numbered one through three, and in three separate envelopes. "Open these in order if you run up against a problem you don't think you can solve," said the outgoing CEO.

Business was running smoothly for the new CEO, but six months later, sales took a downturn, and he was catching a lot of heat. About at wit's end, the CEO remembered the three procedures. He went to his drawer and took out the first envelope. The simplistic instruction read, "Blame your predecessor." So he called a press conference and tactfully laid the blame at the feet of the previous CEO. Satisfied with his comments, the press—and Wall Street—responded positively, sales began to pick up, and the problem was soon behind him.

About a year later, the company was experiencing a slight dip in sales combined with serious product quality problems. Having learned from his previous experience, the CEO opened the second envelope. The instruction simply read, "Reorganize." This he did, and the company quickly rebounded.

After several consecutive profitable quarters, the company once again fell on difficult times. The CEO went to his office, closed the door, and opened the third envelope—the last available procedure. The message said, "Prepare three envelopes, reinsert the three procedures, and issue to your replacement."

What the Heck Is an Audit?

It's a gift

Its two days before the quality audit, and as the Texans say, "This isn't my first rodeo." My team has done an outstanding job to help me and the production team prepare. I'm at my desk looking over the auditor's schedule and audit scope, and finalizing in my head the conversations I'll have to reassure each production manager across the different departments.

There are three light knocks at my open door, a signal that an uneasy soul is about to enter my office. Having an open-door policy means I rarely hear a knock, let alone three. I guess the audit schedule will have to come second for the next few minutes. I look up to see the door frame filled with the sizeable bulk of one of the production supervisors. He does cast a big shadow due to his massive height, and he is as broad as he is tall.

"Hey Iain, a very good evening to you," I say. "Are you here to ask me what the colors of my socks are?" It's a little joke between us; he gets a giggle from finding out which colorful and humorous punk socks I'm wearing that day.

He smiles. "I'm sure you'll make me guess like you always do, Paul," he replies. "But I've got a question for you."

"Shoot." (This is a term I no longer like to use now that I'm in the USA because it may produce an undesirable outcome.)

"I know that you and the quality guys are preparing for this audit thing...."

"Yes, that's right. I remember you being involved in the preparation meetings and reviews, which I am grateful for."

"Well, I'm a bit worried, Paul"

I've seen this before, and armed as I am with my vast improvement Ninja weaponry, I've got an answer prepared. "Don't worry, Iain, it's an opportunity for us to learn about ourselves and an opportunity to improve. Please don't see it as a concern. It'll be over before you know it."

"I know that, Paul. You said that at our last meeting."

Oh wow, I think. That wasn't the answer he was looking for. Now I really need to tune into his channel.

"Iain, please take a seat." He sits down, wedging his massive bulk between the arms of the chair. "What would you like to talk about? And what is it about this audit that worries you?"

"The thing is, Paul, what exactly is an audit? I don't think I get it."

Well, dear reader, like me, you may have been asked this question during your quality professional career. If you haven't yet, you will be, and it's a good idea to be prepared with an answer. I thought I'd write down my views of an audit. If they help, perhaps you can pass them on as a sufficient answer to the question.

First, a note to all veteran and professional auditors: I will begin by oversimplifying your role and might express it in a way that you disagree with. I explain the process and your role in this way because I've found it helps those who are unfamiliar with auditing come to grips with it. All letters of complaint received will be answered in 30 working days.

What is an audit?

In its purest sense, and audit is an activity where the real world is compared against a "standard."

Really, is it that simple? Well, in my childlike view of the world, it is. The route or technique used to compare the real world against the standard can be complex and challenging; however, we should be mindful that an audit is just an exercise in comparison.

Let me give you an example: checking your child's bedroom to see if it is "clean." You ask your firstborn if his room is clean, and he says that it is. You check for yourself, and view a scene resembling the effects of a tornado tearing through a toy store. This is not clean in your opinion, because you have a different standard that defines clean. And so you point out to your child that the multiple dinosaur-shaped hazards lying in wait to trip you do not conform to the definition of clean. Congratulations: You have now conducted an audit.

In the business world, our standards can be specifications, procedures, requirements, or recognized conditions. Due to certain legal requirements—for example, tax laws—financial institutions, financial professionals, or accountants will put huge resources in place to ensure that the rules are followed. Should something arise out of this financial audit that would question the integrity of what you provided the auditors in your accounts, the consequence would be painful: a fine or jail time.

What is a "quality" audit?

As with finance, the business world has rules, requirements, or specifications that define how an organization will produce a "quality" product or service for its customers. A quality audit is a confirmation that the quality requirements are being complied with.

Really, is it that simple? Again, yes it is, and like the financial world, quality auditors must have some level of recognized professional status. The International Registrar of Certified Auditors (IRCA) is a good source for information about auditor certification. I won't go into depth here about audit training or provide a preference to certification; however, I would advise that you, along with your employer, do thorough research on the appropriate training or certification agency. There is no one magic bullet or easy answer for training or certification in general, but I will always recommend applying the plan-do-check-act (PDCA) process to your recognized need.

In the simple world that I live in, I see only four distinct types of quality audits: the internal audit, the supplier audit, the certification audit, and the customer audit.

The internal audit. Typically, this is where one department will visit another and check that department against the company's or customer's requirements. This is useful because it has a level of independence from the processes being audited. Internal audits usually are conducted by part-time auditors in your business, unless you are lucky enough to have a team of full-time, in-house auditors. I used to do internal audits a great deal when I was conducting lean Six Sigma projects. Before starting to improve any process, I would check if the process was at variance to what was defined. I can't tell you the number of improvement projects I'd postpone on the grounds that the process wasn't being followed.

The supplier audit. This is the audit I dislike the most. With this one, an "audit" is demanded of a supplier when it fails to deliver a quality product. If this happens to you, take a time out and work with the supplier on the root cause of the problem before deciding on an audit. Try turning it into a positive experience, and take your specifications with you to see how, through an audit, your supplier is working toward achieving your requirements. If planning a supplier audit, and if time is limited, I would advise not auditing their entire quality management system, and focus on the areas where you see issues. For example, if the components the supplier provides to you repeatedly have problems, and there are many dimensions to the problem, consider spending some time on the components measurement or inspection processes. I like to get a sense of a supplier's maturity by auditing its investigation process, comparing its investigations and the robustness of its corrective actions. To me, this is an indication of the company's ability to improve, and their worthiness to be a supplier. As a Quality Punk, that does make me a demanding customer.

The certification audit. This is the process where third-party auditors will visit your facility and look through your quality management system, and the internal audits that have been conducted within your business, to see if your organization meets the requirements of the standard to which you are seeking certification. In my experience, the third-party certification auditors are full-time professionals with extensive careers in quality auditing. These auditors are good for a reason, so during a certification audit, stay close to them. Stay close not to divert them or try to answer all the questions they pose but to learn from them. I like to remind these certification auditors that I'm paying them a vast amount of money for their services, and I want to get value for the money. I usually get a positive reaction to that request.

The customer audit. This is my ultimate favorite, but only if it's planned correctly. If the customer comes to audit you against their requirements, this is gift. They are going to highlight where you need to improve to meet their expectations. I would happily receive 10 audit findings, rather than have one complaint leading to an unhappy customer.

So, after grossly oversimplifying every element of auditing, I fully anticipate a barrage of complaints highlighting my errors from professional auditors. But because an audit is a brief experience, I don't want to labor the point; I just aim to get to it.

I've experienced many audits in my career, and in preparation for them all I took the same view: Treat audits as an improvement opportunity, as they typically are the "C" in the PDCA cycle. Think about the last audit you had or conducted, recognize the positive outcomes your business gained from it, and share that experience with a colleague. If we recognize the good that comes from audits, the next audit you prepare for may not run up against as much resistance.

What the Fukushima Is a Risk Assessment?

Or, how the Fukushima disaster could have been prevented

On Friday afternoon of March 11, 2011, an earthquake of 9.0 magnitude was detected about 45 miles off the coast of Japan. One of the most powerful ever recorded; it moved the 8,000 square-mile island of Honshu 8 feet to the east. It also set off a 130-ft tidal wave (the same height, ironically, as the world's tallest water slide in Brazil).

Travelling at 70 miles an hour, the wave surged four miles inland, destroying or washing away everything in its path. To this day, substantial debris, like a Harley Davidson motorcycle, continues to wash up on the western shores of Canada and the United States.

The World Bank called it one of the most expensive natural disasters of all time. Certainly it was costly to the estimated 16,000 people who lost their lives.

Already some of these facts are slipping from our collective memory, but most people will continue to associate this earthquake with the subsequent disaster at Japan's Fukushima Daiichi nuclear power station.

After a year of hard work containing the various issues at the plant, a report (NAIIC - The National Diet of Japan The Fukushima Nuclear Accident Independent Investigation Commission) was released to the world. "How could such an accident occur in Japan, a nation that takes such great pride in its global reputation for excellence in engineering and technology?" asked the chairman of the investigating committee. This is a very powerful question and prompts me to ask myself why I'm now reading the report. How can my company benefit from me reading it?

I don't know if you're involved in reviewing your company's internal reports of failure investigations. I'd like to think you're familiar with an investigation process that requires your company to get to the root cause of a problem or issue. I'd even go so far as to presume that you use techniques, such as the 5 Whys, to help you get there.

But let me jump to the conclusion of the six-month investigation of the Fukushima disaster, where the root cause lies: "Therefore, we conclude that the accident was clearly manmade," states the report. I have to say I struggled with this. An earthquake that, in an instant, erased buildings and access to the plant? A mega-wave that overcame the 13-ft sea defense at the site? These were somehow "manmade?"

"What the Fuk-ushima?" I'm thinking. I'm compelled to read on to discover the reasoning behind this statement.

"The operator, the regulatory bodies, and the government body promoting the nuclear power industry all failed to correctly develop the most basic safety requirements—such as assessing the probability of damage, preparing for containing collateral damage from such a disaster, and developing evacuation plans for the public in the case of a serious radiation release," the report explains. Now I see it: The manmade element is coming from the *assessment* of the disaster.

"In addition, although the Nuclear Safety Agency and the operator were aware of the risk of core damage from tsunami, no regulations were created, nor did the operator take any protective steps against such an occurrence," the report continues. "Since 2006, the regulators and operator were aware of the risk that a total outage of electricity at the Fukushima Daiichi plant might occur if a tsunami were to reach the level of the site. They were also aware of the risk of reactor core damage from the loss of seawater pumps in the case of a tsunami larger than assumed in the Japan Society of Civil Engineers estimation. The regulatory bodies knew that the operator had not prepared any measures to lessen or eliminate the risk, but failed to provide specific instructions to remedy the situation."

In summary, this "manmade" disaster was a failure in the manmade risk assessment process. It's all down to this thing called a "risk assessment." If you're unfamiliar with this quality improvement technique, I recommend you learn about it; it's a powerful prevention tool. In the meantime I'd like to advise you on how to tell a good risk assessment from a poor one.

If you're familiar with safety risk assessment, you'll probably know it's also called a "quantitative risk assessment." I'll use this to help explain risk assessments. In a quantitative risk assessment, the risk (R) is calculated from two elements: the impact of the loss (I) and the probability that it will happen (P). Most government health and safety agencies will have their own defined process, or matrix; the Health and Safety Executive (UK Health and Safety Executive) in the United Kingdom will even give you templates for free.

The risk assessment process takes participants through a set of assumptions and uncertainties, which are all considered through a brainstorming-type exercise. The risk will be calculated from the impact value, multiplied by the probability. Or in mathematical terms: $R = I \times P$. If we apply this equation to, for example, the risk of being run over when crossing the road in New York during rush hour, the impact (i.e., being run over by a car) could be very high. However, the probability could be very low (cars don't move very fast during rush hour). But knowing there is a terrible outcome to this scenario, we come to the most important part of the risk assessment: mitigating the risks. To reduce the risk of being run over in New York, the city provides safe crossing zones, or installs walkways and overpasses to physically separate pedestrians from the traffic.

In the case of Fukushima, Chairman Kurokawa is very critical of the mindset that failed to address the mitigating actions to the known risks. Interestingly, his report looks beyond the regulators and the operator to Japan as a society: "The consequences of negligence at Fukushima stand out as catastrophic, but the mindset that supported it can be found across Japan," he writes. "In recognizing that fact, each of us should reflect on our responsibility as individuals in a democratic society." Kurokawa implies that Japan as a nation failed to address the actions required to mitigate the risk. I find this aspect of risk assessment—addressing the mitigating actions—is often forgotten. But it is always the most crucial part of the assessment process.

Please don't be lulled into thinking that a risk assessment is complete when all sections of the form are filled in; it's certainly not yet finished. That happens only when you have put in the preventive measures and tested them for efficacy. This is where the Fukushima disaster really began, not at the time of the earthquake or tidal wave, but at the exact moment of inaction about preventive measures.

And this is the difference between a good risk assessment and a poor one: following through with the identified actions.

When considering the terrible event at Fukushima, or any other major disaster, it's not the known failings or awful headlines that matter, but what we as a society must do to prevent the disaster from happening again. It's clear to me the "manmade" error that led to the failure of the nuclear plant's safety systems was a failure to address the known risks and implement appropriate prevention measures.

So the next time you run up against little management support in implementing your mitigating actions from a risk assessment, remember this was the same mindset that created the disaster at Fukushima. And keep in mind that preventing a disaster from happening is a much more comfortable feeling than having to explain why you did nothing to stop it in the first place.

My Toyota Dilemma, Part Three

The journey toward lean is never-ending

I'm back, writing about another Toyota dilemma of mine. In part one, interestingly titled "My Toyota Dilemma," I wrote how I, as an avid fan and supporter of the Toyota Production System (TPS) have never owned a Toyota. I ended that column vowing I would use Toyota's greatest gift—the 5 Whys—to help find my next car.

In the highly imaginatively titled "My Toyota Dilemma, Part 2," I went on to explain how I bought a Toyota after moving to the United States (thus solving my first dilemma), and the fascinating things you learn when you pull the dash apart and replace it, although you have the mechanical skills of a newborn water vole. Part two ended with a new dilemma, about how I could attend a Toyota plant tour. This is the story of that Toyota visit, and it ends with—you guessed it—me walking away with another "Toyota dilemma."

On a Thursday evening once a month, the Baton Rouge section of the American Society for Quality (ASQ) holds a meeting that I very much like to attend. Although not a member of the ASQ, I'm always welcomed, and I value the meetings when I'm able to make one. I'm a great believer in networking, and if you have never attended this professional institute's meetings, please do so. Perhaps you, like me, will become more than a spectator and get involved as a volunteer.

During one of the earlier sessions I attended, a gentleman by the name of Gary Lane, a lean consultant, provided a detailed PowerPoint presentation of lean's tools and techniques. "Lean companies will always welcome visitors, to let you see how well they do," he noted, and, "Take the opportunity to visit a lean company." He's right: Any company proud of its systems would want to show them off with much pride.

I live in southern Louisiana, not traditionally known for its manufacturing base, and neither does it support any large-scale, lean automotive bases. In the United States, Ford, Chrysler, General Motors, and Chevrolet are headquartered in the north, which is perhaps a bit too far (and expensive) to take a team for a factory visit to learn about quality principles. Granted, I have been to the Tabasco sauce factory 20 miles from my home, which is without a doubt world-class, but world-class manufacturing principles as seen in a completely alien industry might be a little challenging for some to grasp. Watching a little bottle of red sauce spinning past a colleague and explaining about FIFO is all well and fine, but because it's not a piece of equipment the size of a house, or one a team sees every day, it can be difficult to apply the principle in one's home industry, so to speak.

After the ASQ presentation, I spoke with Gary about this and mentioned my desire to visit a lean automotive factory. At that point a warm smile spread across his cheerful face. "Toyota has a mega-factory in San Antonio," he said.

I have been to San Antonio before, about four years ago. My wife and I vacationed on a ranch not far from the city, and we day-tripped the Alamo. However, I wasn't aware of the Toyota factory, or that you could visit it. I remember the ranch vacation was pleasurable, but I think it would have been enhanced by a trip to Toyota. My wife would have probably thought otherwise. So from the comfort of my man cave, I did my research and learned that Toyota did offer scheduled tours at its Texas plant. It even has a visitor center there. I think I did let out a squeal of excitement when I learned about this.

The day after my many hours of planning a Toyota tour, I had a bathtub full of reasons why I had to take a group from the office to the plant. I needed these many reasons to persuade my boss that he should approve the idea and budget it. So I headed to the office and cornered him:

"Scott, I would like to talk over a proposal for a learning opportunity for a group from the base. This would involve going to see Toyota's world-class manufacturing in San Antonio—"

"Good idea, Paul," he said. "We'll start making arrangements."

I wish all my business proposals were accepted that quickly. To be honest, I was lucky: There was a recruitment fair in the San Antonio area that my company was attending at the time, which was already budgeted for.

So on a glorious Monday afternoon, seven of us left Louisiana to go to San Antonio. The plan was to attend the job fair on Tuesday and Toyota on Wednesday morning, returning home the same day. The fair was good; we found some very high-potential candidates, and in the afternoon I took the opportunity with one of the operations managers to visit the Alamo and buy Mexican wrestler masks from the market. The unnamed operations manager claims he bought the mask for his son, but we both know it was an adult-sized mask. However, I do understand the unwritten wrestler's code and will never reveal your identity, *El Salsa*.

I couldn't wait until Wednesday. I have been to automotive factories before, but the thought of seeing trucks being assembled made me even more hyperactive than normal. After checking out of the hotel, I was so adrenalized I forgot that half of the team was in the car behind, following my lead, and I left them in the dust somewhere in downtown San Antonio.

On the southern periphery of San Antonio, the Toyota factory is so immense it took us 10 minutes to drive from one gate to the next and arrive at the visitor center. This is where the lesson in TPS began. As a student of TPS, and having worked for a world-class company where many of the TPS principles were applied, there is perhaps little I don't know, or I should say, little I wouldn't recognize about lean techniques in action.

As we travelled through the center, there were improvement terms, such as *kaizen*, with their definitions in 2-ft-high letters on the walls. There were stations to practice your assembly skills, shadow board principles, a 6-ft display case of awards, and even a station to pull the *andon* cord to stop the process. Apparently there were cars and trucks to look at as well, but I missed these small details once my Improvement Ninja senses caught the scent of excellence.

Being the excitable child that I am, I even stopped and interviewed the very helpful staff. I learned that all the employees at the visitor center came from the manufacturing side. They had to interview for the position, and it was treated as an honorable placement in another Toyota department. Even better, they all loved their jobs at Toyota, not to mention the incredible benefit packages they get for working there.

From the visitor center, we drove in convoy to the factory, where we would see the assembly process. After we donned our safety equipment and headsets, we set off in the back of a golf cart. Within the site we snaked through all the different production areas. I easily identified key lean principles, a secret, hidden-from-view *kaizen* area, clear visual management, and *andon* cords being pulled everywhere.

We were returned to where we started, and we departed for the long drive home. Although I had known what to look for and recognized many practices, as we headed back to Louisiana I learned some valuable lessons about the experience from our team. The car was full of conversations: "Did you see this?", "How could we apply that?" and, "How do you think they got the point of doing that?" Great debates ensued on what we could adopt and strive for; however, I said very little. I just sat back and loved every moment.

I learned that for some in the team who had never been exposed to world-class manufacturing, the tour was an eye-opener. A revolution in thinking akin to taking someone from the Middle Ages to the space station and proving the Earth is, in fact, round. Some had difficulty taking it all in, or even recognizing the basic tools or process of getting to lean. I learned that one tour is not enough because there is so much sensory overload that it is overwhelming.

So I have been presented with my new Toyota dilemma. Oh yes, I will have to extend this series of articles, dear reader. As with any journey toward world-class or lean, it is never-ending, but we must always stride toward it. My dilemma now is based on my observations from this trip. How do I design the next visit where my team can get more from the tour? I'm heading off to my man cave now to start applying scientific principles to factory touring.

The author (second from the right) with his management team, together in the Toyota Texas visitor center.

Six Tips for Avoiding the PowerPointless

Have you ever been taught the skills to use this tool effectively?

Let me give you my definition of "PowerPointing": To provide a presentation of slides so crammed with text that the background no longer shows, and that are read aloud, line by line, by someone staring at a screen rather than the audience. Many of you have experienced this; often the presenter will try to outdo his previous performance by adding yet more slides to read aloud.

If I was working with a dangerous piece of equipment, I'd like to think I would be taught the hazards associated with it. Why haven't we shared with fellow business professionals the hazards associated with PowerPoint?

PowerPoint is an interesting product; it's one of the few examples I can think of where an item's brand name has become synonymous with the act of using it. For example, in Great Britain, the act of vacuuming is often called "hoovering," although personally I prefer the term "vacuuming." Why? Because it sounds like I'm undertaking an action-hero type activity, as in, "I am about to create a vacuum in the man cave!" Besides, as an action hero like Spiderman, I could give needlessly boring presenters the death-ray stare, turning them to dust for abusing the power of PowerPoint.

According to Microsoft's website, PowerPoint is "presentation software that helps you tell a powerful story and share your slides." So really, PowerPoint is just a tool, but like most tools, it can be used incorrectly. I like to compare it to a vernier-caliper measurement device, which can be used improperly as a wrench rather than to indicate where a measurement lies when it is in between two marks on a main scale. OK, so that's not the best analogy I've ever used. My point is that using any tool differently from its intended purpose may not lead to your desired outcome.

I've learned to use PowerPoint the hard way, by working with businesses where presenters delivered truly awful presentations. In addition, I attended a presentation training course many years ago. I'd like to share some golden nuggets of PowerPoint wisdom for the Quality Punks among us.

Tip 1: Stop using PowerPoint and that big screen

What? Stop using PowerPoint? That's crazy talk! Maybe so, but you *can* stop using it for presentations. Be brave and toss that security blanket aside. Years ago, as a Black-Belt-in-training, it was my turn to present my improvement project to the executive leadership team. I'd spent a huge sum of the company's money on development and testing, and it was time to show what I'd accomplished. Back then, when Black Belts were given face time with senior leaders, it was usually at the end of the day—a day of nonstop meetings.

I learned about my day's-end time slot a few days prior. I knew the leadership team would already have been held captive through many PowerPoint presentations. How could I keep their attention, yet make my point effectively? During the dark hours of the night before my presentation, this question still confounded me. But just as I reached the floating point of drifting into sleep, I got the answer: No PowerPoint today.

The next morning I rounded up the operators and engineers to strip down the machine I had been doing the testing on. They stripped it down to its component parts and put these into little plastic trays. We pushed component-burdened trolleys through the corridors, the little wheels squeaking as we rushed to the conference room. Once inside we lined the trolleys up against the wall. Eight well-groomed backs of heads swiveled and turned into faces of disbelief.

"Good evening, gentlemen," I nervously chirped, realizing the big top boss was there. "If I can ask you all to stand up and please come over here." I proceeded to pass out the components, showing the "before" and the "after," all of which were covered in a brothy soup of coolant and oil. Each highly paid executive was captivated, even transfixed, as I handed them gooey metallic parts. No doubt a certain director still remembers me for ruining his beautiful wool suit.

However, I had captured the attention of busy, important people in a way they weren't expecting. I made my presentation; I got the recognition for the improvements and further support from the top, all without a screen, all without a computer, and all without PowerPoint.

Tip 2: Learn presentation skills from the masters

Who would these masters be? Interestingly enough, we are bombarded with expert presenters every moment of the day. Tune in to a news show or log on to the Internet. Look for sports presenters or news readers, particularly those who aren't reading from a teleprompter. I like to observe how they move from one topic to another and how they talk directly to you; they're not reading from a screen somewhere behind them. Consider how your favorite TV presenter would deliver your presentation and use that as a template to improve your style.

Tip 3: Keep it simple, stupid (the KISS method)

Less is sometimes a whole lot more in a presentation. I prefer to have more pictures and fewer words. The reason being that, as a listener, I have an awful habit of reading the text and forgetting what the presenter is saying. I'm more interested in the content than the showmanship. (Incidentally, the KISS method should not be confused with the stage tricks of the glam rock band of the same name. I would not recommend painting a black and white star on your face, or shooting pyrotechnics from your codpiece, unless you are making a presentation to the company's CEO. In that case you have my blessing.)

Tip 4: Poker-player presentations

Look to your audience for "tells" about your presentation in the same way a gambler looks for weaknesses in his opponents. Death-ray stares are a good indication that you may not be getting your point across; on the upside, at least you're making eye contact. If you can get a sense of your listeners' comprehension by observing their body language, it may help you change the tone, pace, or direction of your presentation.

Tip 5: Video yourself making a presentation

OK, this can be embarrassing. However, er, it's not until you, er, videotape yourself that you realize, er, you have funny little, er, quirks, like saying "er" over and over, similar to parakeet speak. By recording and watching your presentation, you can see your style from the audience's point of view. I did this once, and now I can't help but notice when I start doing the er-bird routine.

Tip 6: Practice

Not all of us are lucky enough to deliver presentations frequently and refine our skills. There are social organizations that can help you with your presentation skills, perhaps in a more comfortable environment. If you are passionate about your subject matter, you may feel comfortable talking about it with like-minded people. The next time you are traveling in a vehicle with others, try talking on a subject nonstop for two minutes, without repetition, without pausing, and without saying "er." How about this for your subject: "Why should you work in the field of quality?" A difficult subject, but it will make you think on your feet, which is also a good presentation skill.

What has all this this got to do with quality? I'm sure if the great gurus W. Edwards Deming or Joseph Juran were alive, they, too, would be using PowerPoint to enhance their presentations. For quality professionals like you and me, we are most powerful when we can influence others and help them gain a quality perspective in business. Currently, I'm aware of only one way of influencing others in a respectful and elegant fashion: through communication. Presentations, of any form, are another term for communicating. If you choose to use PowerPoint for your communication, use it to support your message. Don't become overpowered by PowerPoint; be mindful that it is you, and you only, who is the communication device.

It's Easy to Poke Holes in Something

Especially when it already has holes

Cheese is by far one of the greatest foods. It is my only ambrosia, wrapping around my taste buds and sending fireworks of pleasure around my brain. In particular, I love the nutty flavor of Switzerland's holiest of cheeses: Emmental. When you meet me, I will happily bore you into a coma when I start talking about cheese.

Today it isn't Emmental or any other real cheese that has stimulated my quality receptors; it's a management theory that you may be familiar with: the Swiss cheese model (aka "Reason's dynamics of accident causation model").

If you've ever taken part in a failure investigation, you may have seen a diagram, or even produced the diagram yourself, that illustrates all the failure points in the system that produced the undesirable outcome. A perfect storm of a problem, the failure points were precisely aligned in layer upon layer of Swiss cheese slices, creating an aperture through which a bullet could pass without resistance, hitting the failure target.

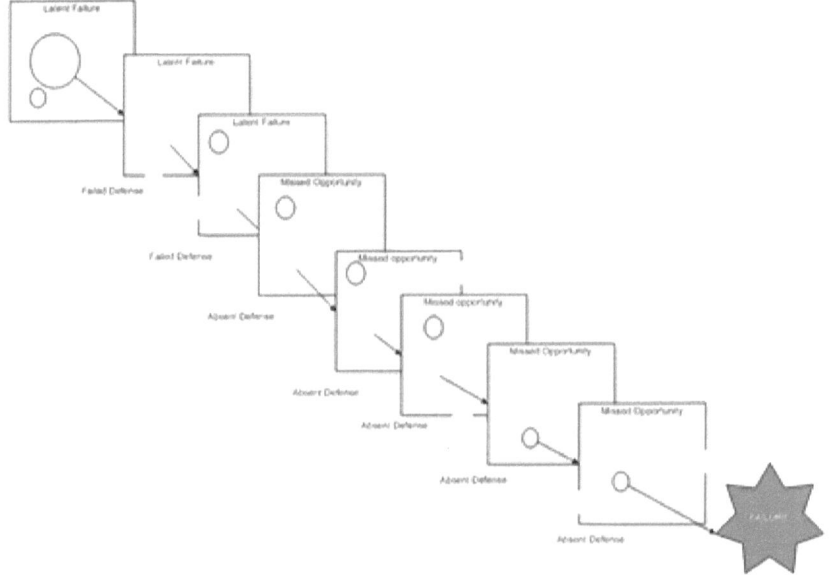

Figure1: Adapted from the "dynamics of accident causation" model, or Swiss Cheese model, (Reason, 1990)

During the 1990s, James Reason, a professor at the University of Manchester in the United Kingdom, did extensive research on the psychology of human nature and wrote a textbook. I refer to his book on a weekly basis. Although he is more of a guru of safety, I firmly believe that Reason's research should be read and applied to the field of general business. And his research should be embraced by quality professionals particularly.

Granted, if you spend time with safety professionals, many will be very familiar with his research. That's because it is used to express many different failings in an accident. However, the Swiss cheese model, as useful as it is to express the causal factors or failures in the defense mechanism, is not the element of Reason's research that aids me in my daily pursuit of excellence. It is something more fundamental; it's Chapter 7 from his book, Human Error (Reason, 1990), "Latent errors and systems disasters."

I attribute my idea or concept of systems' thinking to W. Edwards Deming's teachings. I am a card-carrying member of the Devoted to Deming fan club. At least once a year, I read a book about Deming, or read a book he wrote for the third or fourth time. I now have the ability to recite passages of his work with the passion of a religious leader. Deming introduced to the business world the idea that a business is like a delicate ecosystem, where a small change in one area will effect change across the entire business. He called upon business leaders to pull down the walls between departments, and to let ideas flow openly, to create an environment where everyone works together for the benefit of the company or the system.

Deming's ideas would attribute the failings in a business not to the employee but to a failure in the system that the employee was working in. He recommended focusing on the system, which is owned by management rather than the employee working in the system. This was always a core theme in Deming's philosophy. Deming, however, does have his critics when it comes to systems thinking.

In the book, *False Prophets: The Gurus Who Created Modern Management and Why Their Ideas Are Bad For Business Today* (Hoopes, 2003), James Hoopes writes that Deming's ideas are Utopian and perhaps naive. I also believe that business R&D ideas—or any concept—can or will become antiquated. However, one of the weaknesses in Deming's systems thinking is the fleshy, unpredictable element of any business: the human factor. I believe Deming's concepts can be complemented or enhanced with Reason's research into "human error."

No doubt at this point many proficient quality professionals are throwing down the *poka-yoke* flag on the field of play. I like *poka-yoke*; I like all of Shingo's work; however, mistake proofing does have limitations. It may not always be possible to mistake-proof everything in this world. We are limited by knowledge, engineering, technology, time, and money. Or if you are working in a service business, you are dealing with human decision-making ability. Given these limitations, we will default to relying solely on the human factor—the fallible natural human factor, with more variation, more complexity, or challenges to consistent levels of quality excellence.

When I read an investigation report, nothing grabs me more than seeing the root cause being attributed to human error. I was taught to never accept this and to ask the question: "What caused the human to err?" A good question to ask, but what is the correct answer? This set me on my quest to understand more about human error, and I introduced myself to Reason's work.

If you follow my writing, you may recall that one of my hobbies is to read investigation reports from different industries. I do this primarily as entertainment and to learn. Recently I was made aware of a failure investigation where it was clear that the individual involved knowingly violated the system designed to prevent failure. His company expended a great deal of attention and resources on training, education, competency, technology, procedures, and supervision to prevent a quality problem. In this instance, however, human error was directly to blame. So I asked, what caused the human to err? Granted, I wasn't privy to all the details of the event, but when I reviewed this report, I immediately pulled Reason's book from my library.

In Chapter 7 of *Human Error*, Reason discusses "unsafe acts." In the failure example above, I'll interpret unsafe acts as "acts that lead to poor quality." In section 10.2.4, Reason writes, "An unsafe act is more than just an error or a violation—it is an error or a violation committed in the presence of a potential hazard." Therefore if the hazards of poor quality are present when a poor-quality act is done by an individual, it will only lead to an undesired outcome. The slices of Swiss cheese have aligned, and the bullet has passed through without deflection.

134

In the same section, Reason published a model that describes this graphically and more simply than I can express in writing:

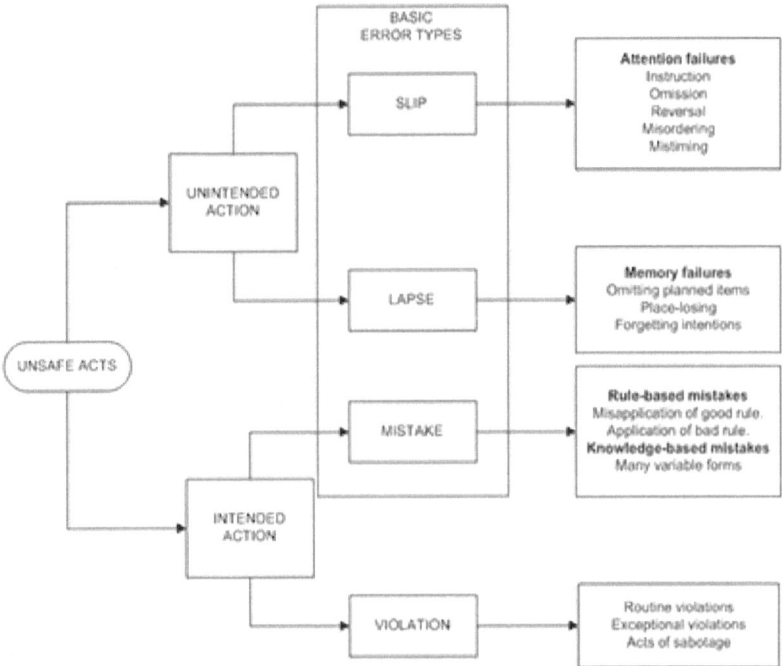

Figure 2: James Reason's summary of the psychological varieties of unsafe acts, classified initially according to whether the act was intended or unintended, and then distinguishing the errors from violations— (Reason, 1990).

So what would my learning be from this investigation and research? We all have this thing called "decision making" or "free will," and it is here I recommend that this has to be addressed. If we can help people make better and more informed decisions in the presence of poor-quality hazards (presuming poor-quality hazards cannot be eliminated), then we will prevent an undesired outcome. Some call this culture change; others see it as systems thinking. I view this as maturity.

All companies or businesses are on a journey; the learning business will thrive and develop, or as Deming put it, "Institute a vigorous program of education and self-improvement." Deming's desire for education will bring organizational maturity, and therefore change, in the culture.

I'm not trying to make the point that Deming was there before Reason, or Reason has bettered Deming, or talk about systems thinking. I am highlighting the point that applying a scientific approach will enhance your thinking and business philosophy, and the effects will be long-lasting. After all, it took 300 years before Einstein improved on Newton's theories of the physical universe.

Reason has been quoted as saying, "You cannot change the human condition; however, you can change the conditions that humans work in." Why not change your condition, and apply some education or self-improvement today? I highly recommend looking up James Reason's body of work.

The Real Men Who Built America

A modest proposal for the History channel—and quality managers

My Tuesday evenings have recently been filled thanks to the entertainment provided by the very nice people at the History channel. I've been thoroughly entranced by the show, The Men Who Built America (History Channel). Production quality aside, it's really an incredible feat, on reflection, how a TV channel could founder so spectacularly in presenting a "reality show" purporting to be a documentary.

As the History channel describes the program on its website: "John D. Rockefeller, Cornelius Vanderbilt, Andrew Carnegie, Henry Ford, and J. P. Morgan rose from obscurity and in the process built modern America.... These men created the American Dream and were the engine of capitalism as they transformed everything they touched.... Their paths crossed repeatedly as they elected presidents, set economic policies, and influenced major events.... Using state-of-the-art, computer-generated imagery that incorporates 12 million historical negatives, many made available for the first time by the Library of Congress, this series will bring back to life the world they knew and the one they created."

What the History channel doesn't state is that intertwined with computer graphics and questionable acting are accounts from historical biographers and interviews with today's political figures or entrepreneurial moguls, all giving their take on the particular man focused on during an episode.

So far I've been entertained, although not particularly well educated, and this vexes me. I don't need the violence, the soap operettas of vendettas between Rockefeller and Vanderbilt, or one-dimensional actors. I yearn for knowledge.

Believing that there may be a desire at some future time to produce a series on the work and lives of my favorite quality gurus has driven me to write an open letter to the History channel:

Dear History Channel Producers,

I like your television station. I like your programming. However, I would like to recommend that if you have funding for a follow-up to the series, *The Men Who Built America,* you consider presenting the quality gurus who lived during the 20th century as the next group of "men." This subject is under-reported or discussed in mainstream media; however, their ideas have massive implications in today's society.

Although following statisticians or management thinkers may not seem to be a great subject to re-create, it would celebrate a group of Americans that, through their timeless ideas, had a greater global impact beyond the borders of America than is often recognized here. These business ideas are more applicable today than ever before, and perhaps by presenting this series about the quality gurus, the History channel might become at least indirectly responsible for helping the global economy recover.

As a self-proclaimed quality punk and improvement *ninja*, I would be available to consult, or even appear as a spokesman, on the series, but only if the following conditions are met:

1. When using special effects to take the viewer back to the period when the quality guru was at his peak, they should be similar in nature to an over-the-top superhero movie. I would like car chases, space robots, and explosions. I wouldn't be too put off by a laser gun battle, either. If the budget isn't available for this, I would be happy to focus on the "men" themselves.

2. The actors must be selected from a pool of trained Shakespearian professionals. I would like to see Patrick Stewart of *Star Trek* fame as Joseph Juran, and Anthony Hopkins as W. Edwards Deming. Actors of this stature could easily give gravitas to their roles. In addition, with their British accents, it is possible that the show might then appeal to a wider female audience. Should you choose to portray *Quality Digest's* Dirk Dusharme or Mike Richman as characters, I would recommend auditioning a Wookie and an Ewok, respectively, for these roles. I say this with all due respect; however, both Wookie and Ewok would have to be strategically shaven to become the spitting images of Dirk and Mike.

3. Location shoots: I will happily consult on filming locations. I only fly economy, and therefore this can save some money toward actors' fees. For more money-saving ideas, I must note that I can provide my own phone and translation app, necessary for translating my Scottish-English into Americanese. This device would prove invaluable when travelling throughout the United States, Japan, China, and Europe.

4. When pitting the men against each other, rather than having the actors exchange glares, perhaps the script could be written to show them meeting and collaborating, as per the foundations of the quality principles they taught.

5. Footage from the past: My genius idea of selecting 20th-century icons of the quality age means there is plenty of photographic and video footage available for inclusion.

Much of this can be easily researched from the Internet. This I can assist with; however, if you could please provide a new iPad and pay my Internet fees during production, I would be most grateful.

6. Selecting the director will be critical to the series' success. My preference would be Steven Spielberg because, as you know, he can delicately convey a story with such beauty that it will tug on the heart strings of all ages and become an instant classic. Appreciating that he may be a little busy, I'd also suggest martial arts movie master John Woo from Hong Kong.

Yours,
Paul Naysmith

I remember the days when documentaries had an educational element to them, rather than an entertainment focus. Although I'm happy to let a historian explain, for instance, the brutalities of our medieval past, I'm not so happy to have it graphically thrust directly into my retinas. Perhaps my ideas of what constitutes a good documentary are outdated, but I realize my work methods shouldn't be as limiting as my ideas.

In his book, The New Economics for Industry, Government, Education: Second Edition (Deming, 2000), Deming explained how we all learn in different ways. People may prefer to learn from observing, from doing, from reading, or from being taught. Watching TV comes naturally to most of us, and it is a powerful communication device, but how do you use it at work? Have you created a documentary or a video of the "process" to educate the observational learners?

Recently I was asked to cross the state line and attend a meeting with our insurance brokers. This was to be held in a comfortable board room, in a corporate office in the middle of Houston at the top of a tall office tower. The purpose of the meeting was to discuss our insurance claims and other items. As important as these issue were, I also needed to describe what we were doing to improve our performance and, ultimately, make fewer claims going forward.

Knowing that I couldn't transport these VIPs to my facility, I had to take my facility to them. I did this with a little 15-minute video. (I like to think many of my quality heroes would have done the same.) On a Friday afternoon, I approached one of my team members and asked if he would like to do "some fun stuff." I usually get an apprehensive or unsure "yes" in response. It seems my approach to work is still seen as a little confusing; why would any boss ask someone to do fun stuff? Anyway, we proceeded, and in less than two hours we captured many improvement projects and transformations to our processes. The next day I edited the video, added music, and threw in a special effect here and there.

In the darkened board room, we watched the video. Thankfully, everyone laughed at the humorous parts, and they were appreciative that we had made the video, allowing them to see what and how we make improvements, in the actual setting. Yesterday I received a nice email from our broker's vice president, thanking us for what we are doing. She even put in four exclamation marks at the end of each sentence. I have learned that this approach worked for me, at least in this particular situation. A group of people were able to relate visually to something they haven't actually touched.

For the suggestion I'm about to make, I apologize to my mother, who spent many years pulling me away from the TV. But here goes: Find some video footage online that will help you describe your quality ideas and improve the learning experience for yourself and others. *Quality Digest* has amassed an extensive library of product demonstrations (that sometimes work) and interviews with today's quality leaders. Take a stroll through these files; there may be something to help you out today.

Bibliography

BBC. (n.d.). *Galileo Galilei (1564-1642)*. Retrieved August 22nd, 2011, from bbc.co.uk:
http://www.bbc.co.uk/history/historic_figures/galilei_galileo.shtml

Deming, W. E. (2000). *The New Economics for Industry, Government, Education: Second Edition* . MIT Press.

Encyclopeadia Britannica. (n.d.). *Sir Ronald Aylmer Fisher*. Retrieved August 22nd, 2011, from britannica.com:
http://www.britannica.com/EBchecked/topic/208658/Sir-Ronald-Aylmer-Fisher

Guardian Newspaper. (2011, June 18th). *Workplace pets? It's not as barking as it sounds*. Retrieved July 18th, 2011, from guardian.co.uk:
http://www.guardian.co.uk/money/2011/jun/18/workplace-pets-reduce-stress-raise-efficiency

History Channel. (n.d.). *The Men Who Built America*. Retrieved November 26th, 2012, from history.com: http://www.history.com/shows/men-who-built-america

Hoopes, J. (2003). *False Prophets: The Gurus Who Created Modern Management and Why Their Ideas Are Bad For Business Today*. Basic Books.

Ishikaw, K. (1991). *What Is Total Quality Control? The Japanese Way*. Prentice Hall Trade.

J.D. Power. (2010, January 1st). *2010 Initial Quality Study Results*. Retrieved June 23rd, 2011, from jdpower.com:
www.jdpower.com/autos/articles/2010-initial-quality-study-results/

Kilian, C. (1992). *The World of W. Edwards Deming*. SPC Press.

NAIIC - The National Diet of Japan The Fukushima Nuclear Accident Independent Investigation Commission. (n.d.). *The official report of The Fukushima Nuclear Accident Independent Investigation Commission (Executive Summar)*. Retrieved August 9th, 2012, from http://warp.da.ndl.go.jp:

http://naiic.go.jp/wp-
content/uploads/2012/07/NAIIC_report_hi_res4.pdf

Neave, H. R. (1990). *The Deming Dimension*. SPC Press.

Ohno, T. (1988). *Toyota Production System*. Productivity Press.

Reason, J. (1990). *Human Error*. Cambridge University Press.

Shaun Panther and Ricardo Gomez. (2010). Public Access ICT: A South-
South comparative analysis of libraries, telecentres and cybercafés in
South Africa and Brazil. *Proceedings of the Sixteenth Americas Conference on
Information Systems, Lima, Peru.* , 1-11.

The Henry Ford. (n.d.). *The Henry Ford: Benson Ford Research Center*.
Retrieved August 22nd, 2011, from thehenryford.org:
http://www.thehenryford.org/research/soybeancar.aspx

UK Health and Safety Executive. (n.d.). *Risk Management*. Retrieved
August 9th, 2012, from hse.gov.uk: http://www.hse.gov.uk/risk/

Wall Street Journal. (2011, May 3rd). *Hong Kong Airlines: Kung Fu to the
rescue*. Retrieved July 18th, 2011, from wsj.com:
http://online.wsj.com/video/hong-kong-airlines-kung-fu-to-
rescue/6A4025C1-4E0C-4A5A-B6CF-943FCAA1E4BA.html

Walton, M. (1998). *The Deming Management Method*. Perigee Books.

Index